Something to say

Centre for Information
on Language Teaching and Research

The Centre for Information on Language
Teaching and Research provides a complete
range of services for language professionals
in every stage and sector of education, and
in business, in support of its brief to promote
Britain's foreign language capability.

CILT is a registered charity, supported by
Central Government grants. CILT is based
in Covent Garden, London, and its services
are delivered through a national
collaborative network of regional Comenius
Centres in England, CILT Cymru,
Northern Ireland CILT and Scottish CILT.

CILT Publications are available through all
good booksellers or directly from:

Central Books, 99 Wallis Rd,
London E9 5LN.
Tel: 0845 458 9910. Fax: 0845 458 9912.

SOMETHING
TO
SAY?

promoting spontaneous classroom talk

VEE HARRIS

JAMES BURCH

BARRY JONES

JANE DARCY

CILT
Centre for Information
on Language Teaching and Research

The views expressed in this publication are the authors' and do not necessarily represent those of CILT.

The authors and publisher would like to thank copyright holders for the permission granted to reproduce copyright material, as detailed next to the relevant excerpts.

First published 2001
by the Centre for Information on Language Teaching and Research (CILT)
20 Bedfordbury
London
WC2N 4LB

ISBN 1 902031 86 5

A catalogue record for this book is available from the British Library

Printed in Great Britain by Cromwell Press Ltd

CILT Publications are available from: **Central Books,** 99 Wallis Rd, London E9 5LN. Tel: 0845 458 9910. Fax: 0845 458 9912. Book trade representation (UK and Ireland): **Broadcast Book Services,** Charter House, 27a London Road, Croydon CR0 2RE. Tel: 020 8681 8949. Fax: 020 8688 0615.

Contents

Figures

Tables

Acknowledgements

We are very grateful to CILT and the Teacher Training Agency for funding the project. We would like to thank all our student teachers for the imagination and energy with which they explored in the classroom the ideas discussed in this book. We are also grateful to James Stubbs for letting us into his classroom and for sharing his teaching materials with us. Professor Rosamond Mitchell clarified the research evidence for us and gave us much food for thought. Finally, we are indebted to Irene Bowerbank for patiently typing and retyping various drafts of the book and to Brian Page OBE for his rigorous and thought-provoking comments on the final draft.

Introduction

This book is the outcome of a project, jointly funded by CILT and the Teacher Training Agency, to explore the implications, both for teachers and teacher trainers, of a consultative, draft version of the new publication, *Common European Framework of Reference for Languages: Learning, teaching, assessment (2001)*. As its name suggests, this detailed and scholarly book is designed to enable all those in Europe involved in teaching a second modern language to reflect on and share their practice. It provides common or compatible descriptions through which we can discuss and compare our objectives, our methodology and the assessment procedures we use. Section 6.4 of chapter 6 of the publication sets out *some methodological options for modern language learning and teaching*. For each area (such as pronunciation or grammar, for example) the document lists a number of options, ranging from what we might consider more traditional teaching approaches to those we have come to associate with communicative language teaching. Implicit in the section is the notion that readers identify not only **what** they do but also reflect on **why** they do it.

We decided that our first task was to review these options, looking at:

- those we felt were valuable and were already part and parcel of our teaching approach;
- those that we did not think were helpful for pupils' learning, for what we believed were sound educational reasons;
- those that we thought were valuable and yet had to admit that we were not confident about how exactly to go about them; how to make them work.

A key question that we kept coming back to in terms of helping pupils to acquire another language was this:

> *In general, how are learners expected to learn a second or foreign language (L2)? Is it in one or more of the following ways?*
> *c) by direct participation in authentic communicative interaction in L2*
> (2001, p143)

Although writing is of course a form of communicative interaction, what struck us most was the problem of creating opportunities for such interaction in speaking activities. *Authentic* implied that the pupils really had *something to say*; not something they **had** to say but something they **wanted** to say. And leaving aside tasks such as giving presentations, *authentic* also implied that they would be speaking spontaneously, rather than repeating a well rehearsed dialogue. Recent technological advances have made it easier for pupils to communicate with each other, to say what they want to say via e-mail, but because it is in written form, they do not have to produce the language on the spot; they can draft and redraft their letters. Opportunities for *authentic* verbal interaction seemed harder. Our concerns seemed to resonate with the difficulties we knew many teachers have in meeting requirements such as this in the National Curriculum Programme of Study:

> *5b) using everyday classroom events as an opportunity for spontaneous speech.* (1999, p17)

We felt that as teachers, **we** were now confident about using the target language for most of what goes on in the classroom but that our pupils were not. And yet, classroom interaction is the one of the most valuable sources of *authentic* communication. However hard we try, the classroom is not the railway station or the dinner table!

So we set ourselves the somewhat ambitious task of trying to:

- reappraise the nature of speaking activities within the context of communicative language teaching, as it is currently implemented in England. The timescale of the project meant that we could not hope to explore more radical approaches such as teaching other curriculum subjects through the medium of the target language. We could, however, ask ourselves what opportunities we regularly offer pupils in the typical classroom situation to engage in genuinely meaningful verbal activities both with us and more importantly with each other;
- devise and evaluate materials and activities aimed at fostering such spontaneous interaction;
- provide concrete, practical, step by step guidance both for student teachers and more experienced practitioners.

The structure of the book

We wanted the structure of the book to be designed to allow you, the reader, to start with the chapter that you felt would be most useful for you and then, if you were interested in exploring the ideas further, to proceed to another chapter. Some people might have already experimented very successfully with different ways of fostering spontaneous interaction, in which case chapter 3 or 4 might be an appropriate starting-off point for them. For many others, not least new entrants to the profession, it might pose quite a daunting prospect and they might want to embark gently, so that both they and their pupils could build up their confidence gradually. They might even feel that the later chapters were not appropriate reading for them at this point in their careers. This meant that the book had to be organised around two parallel strands of progression starting not just from what is the most accessible first step for us as teachers but also what is the easiest for pupils to take on board in terms of communicative interaction.

So, we were faced with two complex questions to answer:

- what constitutes pupils' progression in speaking?
- what is the path for teachers to take as they develop their confidence and competence in fostering that progression?

Progression in speaking skills is hard to capture and it is not appropriate to summarise here the extensive research in this area, although some references are made to it in the next chapter. It is certainly not a straightforward, linear process. Pupils can, for example, be accurate in producing single word utterances on familiar topics but completely lost when faced with a new situation. We might want to consider the relationship between a whole range of features such as:

- length of utterances;
- length of interactions/conversations;
- fluency;
- accuracy;
- complexity;
- range of topics the pupil can cover;
- prior familiarity with the topics;
- range of functions that they can use the language to fulfil; from conveying basic factual information to persuading, justifying and expressing emotions;
- range of registers they can use, adapting what they say according to their audience;
- social skills, such as the ability to initiate a conversation;
- strategic skills that are called into play when we lack the words in the target language that we need. These include the ability to rephrase the sentence in order to keep the conversation going, or hesitation markers to give ourselves time to think.

We might also want to consider their ability to listen to and respond appropriately to whatever is said to them or the degree to which a native speaker has to modify their speech in order to make themselves comprehensible!

In the end, for the purposes of this book, we decided to define progression primarily in terms of the degree of support available and the type of task pupils were faced with. We followed the model, familiar to most teachers, of the **3 Ps:** Presentation, Practice and Production of the language. In other words, were they operating within limited and clearly structured tasks where what was demanded of them was predictable and had been presented and practised by the teacher or were they in more open-ended situations where they had much more choice about what they were going to say and how they were going to say it?

This in turn seemed to match indications from OFSTED reports of the kinds of activities where teachers feel most comfortable and those where they feel less secure. Open-ended activities where pupils have to produce and manipulate the language independently and in new contexts appear to be less common than more routine practice tasks. The former type of task may be all the more difficult for teachers to undertake since they are often not built into the scheme of work. So a task-based approach might allow us to establish a possible route of progression for both pupils and their teachers.

To help you negotiate your way through the book, here is a summary of what you will find in each chapter. We suggest that everyone starts by reading chapter 1, *Why bother?*, which outlines the rationale for encouraging spontaneous interaction language (SIL).

Chapter	Pupil progression	Teacher progression
2	SIL during short bursts of pair work in the presentation and practice stages of the lesson.	Getting started, beginning to explore more meaningful activities but within a very familiar teaching approach.
3 and 4	SIL in guided language production tasks.	Moving on but still within the context of the typical scheme of work, where the language is related to GCSE topics, can be predicted by the teacher and the speaking activities are carefully structured and controlled. Chapter 3 sets out some ideas for pair and group work tasks. Chapter 4 explores what happened when we put these ideas into practice in the classroom.
5	SIL in the context of classroom interaction, where who says what is much less predictable and involving greater choice and risk-taking by pupils.	Risk-taking by the teacher, since lessons not only incorporate familiar GCSE topics but also opportunities to exploit everyday classroom routines and respond flexibly to pupils' interests. This chapter looks particularly at how such routines can be used to teach grammar in a more meaningful way.

Of course, this way of defining progression for both pupils and teachers is oversimplistic. Pupils can and should be taking risks even in the earliest stages of their use of the language. There should be opportunities, for example, in the presentation phase of the lesson for pupils to use the target language to negotiate the words and phrases **they** want to learn, since independence lies at the very heart of spontaneity. Furthermore, each of us has our own preferred teaching style so exploiting everyday classroom routines, such as taking the register and setting homework, may seem a safer way in for some than embarking on the kind of problem-solving tasks we describe in chapters 3 and 4. Equally, we will always need some kind of syllabus and relying just on the language inherent in classroom interaction is not enough. Nevertheless, the general principle is to move from the familiar to the less familiar, from structured activities that the teacher can predict and plan for and that provide clear 'scaffolding' for pupils to those more unpredictable situations, to which both teacher and pupils are having to respond spontaneously.

Suggested tasks

As we have indicated, this was a new and challenging area for us, too, and we wanted to involve our student teachers in helping us establish just what was and was not possible in the classroom. For this reason, most chapters include teaching materials and comments from them.

Even so, you may find yourself asking: *yes, but what does this mean for **me** with **my** classes and in **my** particular school?* To support you in answering these questions, you will find that the chapters are regularly interrupted by this symbol:

- Here we suggest tasks that could provide a link between what you have just been reading and your own reality. At times, too, they invite you to relate what you have just read to recent research findings. As teachers, we do not have to reinvent the wheel; we can draw on insights from research to illuminate what is going on in our classrooms. Theory and practice do not have to be two separate entities.

We hope that the book may be a useful guide in the journey we all embark on when we really want pupils to have *something to say*.

1

Why bother?

For us communication has come to mean using language for a purpose beyond that of practising forms.
(Clark 1984, p13)

A spectre is haunting language teaching; Communication !
(Grenfell 1994, p54)

The search for communication

Many of us who were teaching in the eighties were caught up in the excitement of the new Communicative Approach to Language Teaching (CLT). We discussed avidly the importance of trying to recreate the features of *real communication* in the classroom, even inventing acronymns such as PIFCO to remind us of the need for:

P: a genuine purpose for communicating, as the quote from Clark suggests;

I: an information or opinion gap, where one person knew or believed something that the other did not and the gap had to be bridged through language;

F: feedback – an awareness of whether our message had been successfully conveyed and the ability to handle the unpredictability of not knowing what the person would reply;

C: context – the fact that communication does not take place in a vacuum so we need to be aware of the appropriate language to use to a particular audience;

O: outcome – linked to purpose, emphasising that usually something changes as a result of the communication, even if it is only that someone has changed their mind!

We also read Krashen's (1982) controversial theory of language learning and debated the extent to which learning a first language (L1) is or is not similar to learning a second (L2). In particular, it raised the issue of whether the *natural* unconscious acquisition processes that we use to learn L1 or to pick up another language if we are living abroad is a more effective means of learning a language than formal learning, which he suggests plays a minor and sometimes inhibiting role.

And within the Graded Objectives Movement, we devised syllabuses, teaching materials and tests that were, we thought, based on practical situations in which pupils might find themselves in France, Germany or Spain. We identified the functions we thought pupils would need to fulfil (asking for information, persuading, justifying and so on) and the main notions involved (time, place, etc.) Although other skills were acknowledged, we tended to feel that if pupils could communicate successfully orally, we would have achieved a large part of our goal.

And yet, ten years later, Michael Grenfell refers to this notion of communication as a *spectre* and the OFSTED *Review of Secondary Education Schools in England (1998)* tells us that:

> *After a good start as beginners in Year 7, pupils make less progress in Years 8 and 9 in their use of the target language ... Pupils can answer simple questions on matters concerning personal interests or basic transactions but they lack the confidence to take the initiative in speaking. It is rare to hear pupils seeking clarification, such as* What does this mean? *... Pupils speak with acceptable accuracy in routine situations. When required to speak at greater length or in new situations, their accuracy and fluency deteriorate.*

In his *Reflections on inspection findings 1996/7*, Alan Dobson (1998, p1) notes that:

> *Pupils make less progress in MFL in Key Stage 4 than in most other subjects.*

He goes on to explain that in schools where few pupils make sufficient progress, many pupils are usually:

- *limited to single word utterances;*
- *over-dependent on written prompts when speaking;*
- *unable to deal with the unexpected in speech;*
- *incomprehensible to a sympathetic native speaker because their pronunciation and intonation are poor.*
  (p9)

So what is going wrong? It is not the purpose of this book to analyse the reasons. The overemphasis on topics and on transactional situations, the constraints of the GCSE syllabus, the limitations of textbooks that purport to be 'communicative' but all too often stop short of 'the real thing'; these have been graphically described in articles by Michael Grenfell (1994) and Do Coyle (2000), amongst others. And of course, there is the whole issue of the role of grammar that is currently being reviewed. Rather, our intention is to look forward. Paradoxically, some of this will involve going back to the principles of CLT. Without principles, it becomes impossible to generate one's own ideas; we are limited to copying other people's tips. At the same time, we will draw on evidence from more recent research in the hopes that it can help us turn the communicative dream into reality.

If we have somewhat lost our way, it is not surprising. In Britain, the demands of implementing GCSE and the National Curriculum and the pressures of OFSTED inspections have been highly time-consuming. Certainly, the National Curriculum Programme of Study (1999) includes statements that support communicative methodology.

Pupils should be taught:

> *2d: how to initiate and develop conversations;*
> *2e: how to vary the target language to suit context, audience and purpose;*
> *2f: how to adapt the language they already know for different contexts;*
> *2g: strategies for dealing with the unpredictable.*
> (p16)

During Key Stages 3 and 4, pupils should be taught knowledge, skills and understanding through:

> *5b: using everyday classroom events as an opportunity for spontaneous speech;*
> *5c: expressing and discussing personal feelings and opinions;*
> *5h: using the target language for real purposes.*
> (p17)

It is, however, a list of commandments with few examples and no explicit reference to any theories of language learning that may underlie it. What, then, can research tell us? However great the pressures on us simply to survive in the classroom or to ensure pupils achieve good grades, it is worth stepping back and reflecting not just on what we do but why we do it. What are the assumptions underlying our own everyday practice? That is after all what the Council of Europe publication invites us to do.

What can research tell us?

Below and in no particular order are some extracts from current research along with some questions to consider. They are also questions we asked ourselves when we embarked on the project. Taken out of context here, the extracts may seem dry and somewhat abstract. Throughout the book, however, we have tried to relate them to classroom realities. You will find that we often return to them when we suggest the tasks that you might want to undertake, signalled by this symbol:

To make referring backwards and forwards from the research to the classroom examples easier, we will number them. Since not everyone will read the book from start to finish, we will also not adopt the usual convention of using *op.cit.* to refer to books already mentioned, but will provide the date of publication each time.

In selecting short extracts from the various authors' work, we are very aware that we do not do justice to the complexity of thought underlying their research. We hope that the bibliography and the *Ideas for useful follow-up reading* at the end of most chapters will allow you to explore the ideas in greater depth. Each extract ends with questions to consider that may help relate the research to the reality of your own classroom or to your own language learning experiences. They may also invite you to ask your pupils what they make of their language learning experiences, since this kind of feedback is often very illuminating!

Extract 1

> As early as 1989, Richard Johnstone indicated the dangers of *'falling between the two stools',* of promoting neither pupils' fluency nor their accuracy. He suggested that: *there are two complementary sides to communication: one being intuitive and spontaneous, the other being analytical and reflective. It is not unfair to suggest that in many cases current practice in schools is neither spontaneous nor reflective to an appropriate degree. There is still a substantial amount of unspontaneous and unreflective drill and practice, even if nowadays this is geared to functions and notions in context rather than to structures out of context as was often the case in the 70s. This book argues for pulling apart, though not destroying completely, the middle ground that consists of drill and practice. In the one direction, it argues for a move towards less cerebral, more stream of consciousness activity, 'letting it all hang out'... in order to allow language to flow more freely to and from its rich underlying associative sources. In the other direction, it recommends a move towards more analytical reflection, initiated by learners themselves, as they analyse communication problems and develop, test out and modify their ideas on how best to solve them.*
> (1989, p8)
>
> **Question: As a successful language learner yourself, do you agree with Richard Johnstone's view of the two sides of communication? How helpful were drills and practice for you? To what extent did time you spent abroad enable you to let the language flow freely? Can such experiences be recreated in the classroom? How, when and where can these be fostered? What was the role of analytical reflection in your language learning?**

Extract 2

> Rosamond Mitchell's longitudinal study of French teaching in two secondary schools documented the course of linguistic progression of a cohort of sixty 11–13 pupils over a two year period. She noted that: *in all classrooms, the largest proportion of observed time was given to 'practice' rather than to 'communicative activities',* although there was considerable variation from teacher to teacher. She observed three main features of classroom learning; the memorisation of unanalysed chunks of language (such as *je m'appelle*), the monitoring of and reflection on the language itself, and creative construction, where learners experimented with

the language. She goes on: *our learners were explicitly taught a curriculum consisting very largely of unanalysed phrases. Typically these took the form of face-to-face Question and Answer exchanges, clustered around topics such as* the family, hobbies *or* likes and dislikes. *Our independent evidence on learners' progress also viewed this 'chunk memorization' stage as important... But how do children 'move on' from regurgitation of learned fixed phrases to a more creative and flexible control of the target language?It seemed to us that the prime driving force was communicative need, e.g. to extend the reference beyond the first and second person reference typically embodied in the learned Question/Answer formulae. The various problem-solving tasks used in successive rounds of the project elicited rich evidence of children struggling to succeed in finding 'choice points' within learned formulas, where new items could be substituted to fit the communicative demands of the moment.*
(1997, p23)

This process of experimenting with how to break down the chunks, to 'unstick them' is evident in the way that, in the course of the project, one pupil moved from the accurate *comment t'appelles-tu?* to *il s'appelle ...* to *comment t'appelles-tu?* (when she had to ask the name of someone in the picture, rather than to give her own) to *il y a s'appelle, comment s'appelle ... umm ... un garçon?*

Question: Have you noticed your pupils passing through similar phases of progression? In your experience, what pushes them to do so? How do you respond to these phases? Have your learners noticed this is happening? If so, what are their feelings about their progress?

Extract 3

Peter Skehan and Pauline Foster explored the effects on students' language performance of different types of oral task and whether they were given prior planning time or not. They concluded:

Learners required to complete tasks seem unable to prioritise equally the three performance aspects of fluency, accuracy and complexity. Achieving highly in the one seems mostly to be at the expense of doing well on the others ... If there are tensions between fluency, accuracy and complexity, teachers may need to consider how they design instructional activities to achieve progress in each of these areas separately and how they can promote balanced longer-term development in which the three areas do not progress at one another's expense.
(1997, p209)

Question: What responses should the teacher make to errors made during unplanned spontaneous interaction? What responses do you think learners want them to make?

Extract 4

> *I have claimed that many pupils do feel uninvolved when learning language, do not feel they are expressing themselves. Research suggests that when we learn our first language, it is not only a way of getting things done, it is also an expression of sense of self. It is not enough to take in the world that language represents. It is rather necessary to create oneself in and through that language. In other words, language is not something that we access like a baggage of information, taking out the bits and pieces to suit our needs at a particular instant. It is rather the means by which we create sense; of our world, of and for ourselves ... I keep faith with my spectre, but realise that it will only become flesh once we have broken the barriers of topic-based coursebooks in order to allow more freedom for personal identity to come forward.*
> (Grenfell 1994, p58)
>
> **Question: Of course, learning a second language is not the same as learning the first, not least because when we come to learning it we already know the world and are not acquiring new concepts alongside the new words. Nevertheless, many of us feel we have a different sense of identity when we speak the foreign language to when we speak our mother tongue. In what way is it different? What experiences allowed it to grow? Have you asked learners what they feel when speaking a foreign language?**

Extract 5

> Zoltan Dörnyei and Kata Csizér propose: *Ten commandments for motivating language learners.*
>
> *We take the view that L2 motivation is one of the most important factors that determine the rate and success of L2 attainment; it provides the primary impetus to initiate learning the L2 and later the driving force to sustain the long and often tedious learning process.*
>
> Among their ten commandments is the following, with suggested guidelines:
>
> ***Select interesting tasks:***
>
> *Choose interesting topics and supplementary materials;*
> *Build on the learners' interests rather than tests or grades, as the main energizer for learning;*
> *Raise learners' curiosity by introducing unexpected or exotic elements;*
> *Make tasks challenging to involve your students.*
> (1998, p212)
>
> **Question: To what extent does the content of your scheme of work allow you to build on the learners' interests and raise their curiosity? How do you know what interests your pupils?**

Extract 6

There is a growing body of evidence to suggest that there is an urgent need to review the content of communication; i.e. what learners are told to talk, read or write about ... Perhaps it is time to take a serious look at how modern foreign languages might contribute to other areas of the curriculum. This is not to reduce modern languages simply to the service of other subjects but to extend its communicative repertoire, explore its potential for cognitive challenge and to increase its relevance to learners ... How often do we develop reasoning and problem-solving into our repertoire beyond gap-fill timetables and deciding how to get from one place to the other?
(Coyle 1999, pp14,15).

Question: Within the GCSE topics, what potential is there to use the target language to teach pupils something new about the world in which they live or to solve problems? What do learners say they want to learn about?

Extract 7

Pupils who arrive in a new country are faced in school with the problem not only of learning the language but also of accessing the curriculum: science or history, for example. This is clearly a different situation from their indigenous peers. Nevertheless, although somewhat complex, research into bilingual language learning may relate to our instinctive 'gut sense' of what makes something easy or difficult for our pupils. If we want to create genuinely meaningful tasks, as Do Coyle suggests, then this might involve presenting pupils not just with a linguistic challenge, but also a cognitive one. In other words, there would be something they wanted to puzzle out; it would not be simply a matter of whether they did or did not know the words to order food in a restaurant.

Jim Cummins (1984) uses the continuum in Table 1.1. to show how these language and cognitive demands need to be balanced in order for bilingual pupils to develop on both fronts. **Context-embedded** implies that the task is linguistically easy because the information is conveyed through other means than language; for example visual aids, mime and so on. **Context-reduced** means that they have to rely just on the language alone to understand. **Cognitively demanding** tasks require pupils to reflect on their own positions, puzzle out something, use their reasoning powers. **Cognitively undemanding** tasks are straightforward and can be performed almost on automatic pilot. Thus a task in quadrant B would be both linguistically and cognitively challenging, whereas a task in quadrant C would be linguistically easy and possibly not challenging enough. Of course, no task fits fairly and squarely into one quadrant and it is more a question of balancing out the different demands.

Question: What does this mean for us as modern language teachers? If a task is cognitively challenging, how can we adjust it to ensure that it is readily accessible linguistically? Conversely, if a task is difficult linguistically, how can we adjust it to make it cognitively easier? What do pupils say makes something easy or hard?

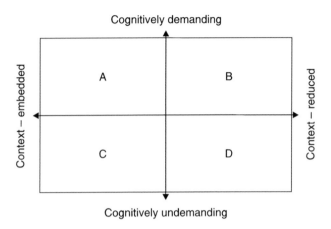

Cognitively demanding

Context – embedded

A   B

C   D

Context – reduced

Cognitively undemanding

Table 1.1. Task demands

Extract 8

Michael Canale (1983) suggested that communicative competence has the following four components:

• Grammatical competence;

• Discourse competence – knowledge of the rules governing the structure of longer texts, whether it is how to make paragraphs in written work 'hang together' or how conversations work – how to turn-take, for example, or to mark that you are moving on to a new point;

• Sociolingistic competence – the control of speech and writing styles appropriate to different situations and audiences;

• Strategic competence – how to cope when what you want to say is beyond your linguistic repertoire but you want to keep the communication going; how to ask for clarification, or use paraphrase, or tone of voice to indicate what you mean.

In relation to discourse competence, Jane Willis (1996) comments: *Through interaction, learners have the chance to acquire the range of discourse skills they need to manage their own conversations ... However, practice activities that are not meaning-focused, such as acting out dialogues, where the main aim is to practise specific forms and functions, have been found inadequate ways of promoting learning by themselves. All too often, learners do them on automatic pilot without really having to think about what they mean.*
(1996, p14)

Question: What activities can we devise that really push pupils to negotiate meaning and develop their discourse competence?

Extract 9

The last twenty years have seen extensive research into what it is that good language learners do that ineffective learners do not. It seems that good language learners (such as language teachers!) automatically (and often unconsciously) use a much wider range of strategies for making sense of the target language whether in reading or in listening than poor language learners. They also seem to know how to get their message across within the limited linguistic resources at their disposal; the strategic competence described in extract 8.

Some people can communicate effectively in an L2 with only 100 words. How do they do it? They use their hands, they imitate the sound or movement of things, they mix languages, they create new words, they describe or circumlocute something they don't know the word for – in short they use communication strategies.
(Dörnyei 1995, p57)

Below is a modified and reduced list of such strategies from his study. There has been some debate as to the extent to which these strategies are teachable or even whether it is necessary to teach them and we can rely on them to develop automatically in response to communicative need. A recent review, however, (McDonough, 1999) summarises encouraging evidence for the potential value of teaching communication strategies.

Question: To what extent do you enable pupils to develop these survival techniques? Are your learners aware of them? If so, which? Have you asked them how they cope in problematic situations?

Strategy type	Strategy	Strategy example
1. Circumlocution	Describing or exemplifying the target object or action.	*The thing you open bottles with* for *corkscrew, maison de poissons* for *shell*.
2. Approximation	Using an alternative term which expresses the meaning as closely as possible.	*Ship* for *boat*.
3. Use of all-purpose words	Extending a general, empty word.	*Thinggie, what-do-you-call-it* as well as the overuse of *stuff, make, do*.
4. Word coinage	Creating a non-existent L2 word based on a supposed rule.	*Vegetarianist* for *vegetarian*.
5. Use of non-linguistic means	Mime, gesture, facial expression, or sound imitation.	

Strategy type	Strategy	Strategy example
6. Foreignizing	Using a L1 word by adjusting it to L2 phonologically (i.e. with a L2 pronunciation) and/or morphologically (e.g. adding to it a L2 suffix).	
7. Appeal for help	Turning to the conversation partner for help either directly (*what do you call …?*) or indirectly (e.g. rising intonation, pause, eye contact, puzzled expression).	
Stalling or time-gaining strategies		
8. Use of fillers/ delayers/ hesitation devices	Using filling words or gambits to fill pauses and to gain time to think.	*Well, you know, now let me see, as a matter of fact.*

Taking up some of Richard Johnstone's (1989) ideas, we might also want to add:

9. Turn-getting gambits	Used to break into a conversation.	*No but listen, yes but …*
10. Turn-giving gambits	To give yourself time to think.	*What do you think? Really?*
11. Picking up on useful expressions	Listening to a person talking to see what words, structures they use and then incorporating them into own speech.	

Extract 11

The extent to which we use such communication strategies may vary according to our personality. This is a complex area but Michael Grenfell and Vee Harris (1993) suggest that one of the reasons communication strategies may be hard to use is because some pupils prefer to '*play it safe*' and will only say something if they are sure it is accurate. Others are more extrovert and have a *desire to 'communicate at all costs'*, regardless of accuracy.

Question: What differences do you notice between pupils' responses to oral tasks? Do you comment on these in school reports and in lesson time? How do pupils identify what they believe they need to do in order to improve?

Extract 12

> Other individual differences in the way pupils tackle learning the language are equally important. Peter Skehan's book (1998) includes a discussion of recent research into preferred learning styles. This is a vast and complex area but it includes differences in preferred modality. **Visual** learners, for example, find written 'props' essential, **auditory** learners find them distracting and prefer to focus on listening closely. As its name suggests, kinaesthetic learners appreciate active, hands-on tasks, often involving some form of body movement. Individual differences also include distinctions between analytic and holistic learners. The first group like to be told the rule from the word go and then work out other examples of it. The second group prefer to be given lots of examples, from which they themselves work out the rule. Other variations include active versus passive learners and so on.
>
> **Question: How can we cater for each pupil's individual needs and preferred learning styles? What do your learners prefer?**

Extract 13

> Brian Page reminds us that a teacher-centred classroom is unlikely to foster genuine spontaneous interaction; he reminds us, too, of the relationship between independent language **use** and independent language **learning**:
>
> *In recent years we have moved towards providing examples of authentic foreign language for learners to work with – signs, brochures, extracts from magazines and newspapers, genuine French, German and Spanish people recorded on audio and video tape. But we still tend in textbooks and in class to give a great deal of support – word lists, explanations, and questions that point learners in the direction we want them to go. How else, we say, will they be able to cope with genuine foreign language? But if we as teachers are to do our job properly, we must give them the means to cope on their own.*
> (1992, p2)
>
> **Question: How can we give learners sufficient confidence and competence to be able to choose both what to say and how to say it; to navigate their own way through the complex and unpredictable nature of the language world around them? How do your pupils respond when faced with opportunities to take control of their own learning?**

Finally, we want to draw on a very helpful personal discussion we had with Rosamond Mitchell, when we embarked on the project. Here is a very brief summary, although not always in her exact words, of the main points that we took away from the discussion.

Extract 14

> The big gap in CLT and its earlier versions was that it actually lacked the language learning theory. It had a big new idea about syllabus which was 'let's go for functions and notions instead of grammar'. I think that what has happened in the last fifteen years is that we have become much more conscious of that dimension and that there is still an issue about how does grammar develop? Basically we need to accept that classroom learning is messy. There are at least three different types of learning going on and it is our responsibility to make sure that we offer pupils a diet of all three:
>
> • I have had to re-evaluate my approach to behaviourism; pupils do need to memorise things like the unanalysed chunks and to revisit and re-use that store of learning;
>
> • there is also a cognitive approach to learning – pupils should be able to spot verbs and know what they do in a sentence. Pushing pupils on to greater accuracy, greater ambition are vital parts of anybody's teaching. Let's re-instate language itself as part of what we talk about, the **content** of our lessons;
>
> • the third area is the kind of experiential, unconscious, mysterious bit associated with Krashen's acquisition theory.
>
> The focus on the last point may have had the effect of 'rubbishing' other kinds of classroom learning, instead of saying 'how do we stick all this together? How do we weave this kind of experiential start with the continuing need to reflect on, analyse and study the language?' If one reflects on CLT in the late nineties, that seems to me to be one of the areas that the original model did not clearly develop.
>
> It seems to me that if your question is about how to get pupils speaking, then the notion of multi-skills is important. We really have to go back to the content of language teaching. Is it the case that language learning is about leisure and tourism and the World Cup? Or is it about intercultural understanding, social inclusion and general educational values? I wonder if amongst your more ambitious activities for the more experienced teacher, you could bring in researching a particular subject for homework and bringing that knowledge to the classroom interaction?

In this brief and oversimplified review of the literature, we have seen some central concerns emerge about the way CLT is currently being implemented:

• the importance of meaning, of having *something to say* that pupils feel is genuinely important for them, that engages them on a personal level both emotionally and cognitively;

• the importance of preparing pupils to cope with real life communicative demands within the limited linguistic resources at their disposal;

• the difference between drills to practise the language and real language use; yet the value of activities that help pupils to memorise language;

• the need to review the place we give to grammar and how we teach it;

- a recognition of *mental overload*, of the limited space in our brains to do ten things at once! This has two immediate implications. On the one hand, we need to acknowledge that it may not be possible amidst the pressures of an instantaneous conversation both to struggle to express what you want to say and to say it with the minimum of error. On the other hand, we need also to recognise the demands of the nature of the task itself – the extent to which it is both linguistically and cognitively demanding or only offers challenges on one front.

In the chapters that follow, we will return to these themes, trying to find a balance between:

• the demands of the GCSE syllabus	• the desire to promote authentic communication
• the need to provide pupils with enough support	• preparing them for the demands of real life communication
• recognition of the value of explicitly talking about the way the language operates	• providing pupils with enough concrete meaningful experiences of the language to begin to unconsciously work out their own rules

We start at the beginning. Chapter 2 sets out how even the presentation and practice phases of the lesson can be made more meaningful.

Before we do so, however, let us visit the classroom. We have said that our focus was on encouraging spontaneous verbal interaction. So it may seem strange that we end this chapter with a letter. It is written by a Year 11 pupil after two years of learning German, with two lessons a week. The letter suggests that giving pupils *something to say* may also have positive side effects on their written work. It also illustrates many of the themes discussed in this chapter.

Liebe Anna!

Ich weiß, daß du mich nicht kennst, deshalb möchte ich mich Dir vorstellen! Ich bin Deine Partnerin für den Austausch und ich heiße Sue. Vor allem bin ich wahnsinnig nett und Kinder und Tiere mögen mich viel.

Ich habe langes, blondes, lockiges Haar und mein Lieblingsessen ist Froschbein in Rotwein gekocht. Wie ist es bei Dir? Vielleicht möchtest Du etwas über meiner Familie wissen? Kein Problem! Ich denke, daß ich ungefähr 10 Geschwester habe. Es ist schwer zu sagen, weil unser Haus so groß ist, daß wir immer uns verlieren. Eigentlich, es ist möglich, daß Tausende von Geschwester habe, weil Vati ein Spender für eine Samenbank ist. Gestern, habe ich sechs Brüder und vier Schwestern zu Frühstück gesehen. Wir wohnen in einer ganz interessanten Stadt, die Lancaster heißt. Lancaster is eine alte und historische Stadt, die in der Nehe dem Seengebiet, der Irischensee und den Yorkshire Dales ist. Es gibt viele alte Gebäude und eine schöne Burg, die steht auf dem steilen Hügel, auf die die Römer eine Festung gebaut haben.

Ich hoffe, daß Du Lancaster sehr spannend finden wirst, und daß Du Geschichte magst.

Jetzt mussen wir über unsere Stundenplan für Deine Besuch sprechen. Die spannendste Aktivität ist am Freitag, wenn wir in die Disko gehen. Ich hoffe, daß Du gern tanzst, oder Du Dich langweilst viel, nicht wahr? Wir haben am Sontag nichts zu tun. Kannst Du mir sagen, was wirst Du gern machen? Schließlich muss ich diesen Brief fertigsein machen, weil ich alle meine Geschwister finden muß, um sie zu zählen. Ich wünsche Dir eine schöne Reise, und freue mich auf, Dir kennenzulernen.

Mit freundlichen Grüßen, Deine Sue.

Dear Anna,

I know that you don't know me and that's why I want to introduce myself to you. I'm your exchange partner and my name is Sue. Above all, I'm incredibly nice, and children and animals like me a lot.

I have got long, blond, curly hair and my favourite food is frogs' legs cooked in red wine. What about you? Perhaps you would like to know something about my family? No problem! I think that I've got about 10 brothers and sisters. It's difficult to say because our house is so big that we are always getting lost. In fact, it's possible that I've got thousands of brothers and sisters because my dad is a sperm doner. Yesterday I saw six brothers and four sisters at the breakfast table. We live in a very interesting town called Lancaster. Lancaster is an old and historic town which is near to the Lake District, the Irish Sea and the Yorkshire Dales. There are lots of old buildings and a nice castle, standing on the top of a steep hill on which the Romans built a fortress.

I hope that you will find Lancaster exciting and that you will like the history.

Now we have to talk about our timetable for your visit. The most exciting activity is on Friday, when we are going to the disco. I hope that you like dancing or else you will get very bored, won't you? We have got nothing to do on Sunday: can you tell me what you would like to do? I have to finally finish this letter because I have to find all my brothers and sisters, in order to count them. Have a pleasant trip and I'm looking forward to getting to know you.

Best wishes, Sue

Figure 1.1. Sue's letter

- To what extent is this a typical GCSE letter?
  - Underline the words and phrases that come straight from GCSE topics;
  - Put a circle round more unusual expressions.
- How does the letter relate to language as a *sense of self*, discussed in extract 4?
- Where are the *unexpected or exotic elements*, advocated in extract 5?
- How does the letter relate to the features of communicative competence described in extract 8?
- What do you think was the process that eventually enabled this pupil to express her own identity and feelings and to invite comments and suggestions from Anna? This is the focus for the rest of the book!

Useful follow-up reading

Full details of the books and articles from which the extracts were taken can be found in the bibliography.

Since the original draft of the book was written, the journal *Language Teaching Research* has devoted an issue (vol.4, no.3) entirely to the theme of tasks in language teaching. The five papers discuss a number of central issues including the effects of affective and social variables on learners' engagement in oral argumentative tasks and the use of L1 during task performance.

2

Starting out: presenting and practising new language

Introduction

We saw in chapter 1 the concern expressed by both Richard Johnstone and Rosamond Mitchell that much of what goes on in modern language classrooms is drilling and practice rather than genuinely communicative activities. How often in real life, for example, do we hold up a pencil or point to a picture of one and ask *is this a pencil or a pen?* Nevertheless, many teachers believe that this type of questioning is a vital stage in the language learning process, allowing pupils to get their tongues round the new sounds and to memorise the new words, without being over-reliant on the written form. Does this mean that such drilling has to be meaningless? This chapter explores ways in which even the presentation and practice stage of lessons can be used to give pupils opportunities to have *something to say*.

Presenting new language to learners in the first two or three years of language learning often involves the use of flashcards, words on the board or textbook page, or pictures/captions on the overhead projector to establish meaning. The role of the class is to listen attentively and often to repeat the language model given by the teacher. Thereafter learners may be asked to listen to a cassette or to read a text where the new vocabulary is repeated, or to answer simple questions orally.

The presentation phase, when the learners meet new language, is vital especially when they are then asked to re-use what they have seen or heard as a class activity or in pairs. If concentration lapses during this initial introduction then they may be unable to complete subsequent activities. In other subjects pupils can turn to a friend and ask what has he or she has missed; in history, or science, for example, the friend can offer quick remedial action and words of advice and the pupil is back on task. In language lessons this is more difficult. As teachers we do, of course, check comprehension by using a number of strategies – pupil as interpreter, matching pictures to captions, ticking appropriate symbols representing meanings of different words or sentences, etc. Rarely do we, however, encourage interaction in pursuit of meaning **as the presentation phase is in progress**. Although we may occasionally provide learners with the language to slow our speech down, or to request us to repeat, (the *appeal for help* communication strategy referred to in chapter 1), seldom do we systematically encourage **and develop** these coping strategies, thereby harnessing their potential to help foster our pupils' linguistic progression. Even less frequently do we give learners the language to express frustration, pleasure, or to ask for a word to be spelt a second time, or that the projector be re-focussed or that an illegible word on the board be spelt aloud or even rewritten. It is with the aim of greater learner participation in the learning process, and increased teacher–pupil and pupil–pupil interaction, that this chapter is written.

We hope to show that the language of participation and interaction can be as important as, or even more important than, the topic-based content of textbooks or more conventional schemes of work. As is the case with all language which learners are expected to use, however, this type of interaction language has to be modelled by the teacher, extended grammatically beyond the set phrase, and used as often as possible across a range of contexts. It also needs time to become part of a pupil's repertoire, so it has to be built into the planning of all lessons in the same way that topic content or grammatical progression is carefully prepared.

To ensure greater learner involvement, and to mirror more what happens in real life language learning we are advocating **making the class struggle to arrive at meaning**. This entails never telling/showing a class anything without their having to interact with the teacher, or indeed with other sources of language input (tape, video, text, fellow pupils, the Foreign Language Assistant (FLA), etc.) in pursuit of meaning. Making the class struggle to arrive at meaning is a device for encouraging the pupils to:

- begin to develop their independence in using the language for themselves and not simply in response to the teacher's questions;
- hypothesise and speculate about potential meaning;
- take risks with language;
- think in the language;
- develop their strategic competence, their ability to cope with the problems of communication that are inevitable when we are trying to learn a new language.

The sections that follow discuss and illustrate how this can happen.

Section 1	the presentation stage, where pupils must struggle to understand the meaning of the new topic language that the teacher is offering them.
Sections 2 and 3	the practice stage, where the often dry routine of memorising the sounds and written form of the words can be turned into a dynamic interaction between teacher and pupil, and pupil and pupil.
Section 4	tackling pronunciation problems which pupils experience, particularly when they are exposed to the written form of the word.
Section 5	revising topics recently covered, often preceding an end of unit test.
Section 6	games where, in contrast to the presentation stage, instead of the teacher, it is the pupils themselves who make each other guess about meanings.
Section 7	the key principles behind the ideas discussed so far.

| Section 8 | what happened when a group of student teachers and their tutor sought to put the principles into practice. |
| Section 9 | a range of *rewards and sanctions* strategies that student and practising teachers have used to motivate more reluctant learners to engage in spontaneous use of the target language. |

Section 1: Presenting new language

Let us imagine we are teaching the following school subjects in French:

Masculine: (in blue)
le français
le dessin
l'anglais

Feminine: (in red)
la géographie
la chimie
la physique
l'éducation physique
l'histoire
l'EMT

1. Contextualising the new vocabulary

The OHT in Figure 2.1. is placed on the screen. Only the central section with the question is shown; the symbols for the subjects are covered up with post-its.

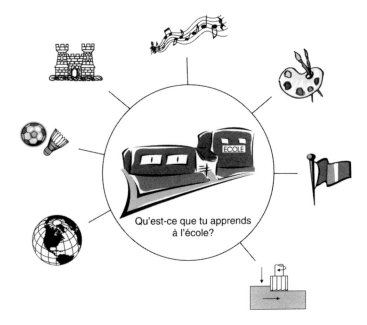

Qu'est-ce que tu apprends
à l'école?

Figure 2.1. OHT of school subjects

The teacher points to the central section of the OHT and says: *On commence quelque chose de nouveau aujourd'hui. Qu'est-ce qu'on va faire, qu'est-ce qu'on va apprendre?* This encourages the class to speculate about what the topic area is. He or she then asks the contextualising phrase, *Qu'est-ce que tu apprends à l'école?*

A contextualising phrase is the phrase, usually a question, that many teachers use to preface the language being guessed in order to ensure that it is presented in a clear communicative context. For example, if it were a café dialogue and food items were being guessed, then these would be prefaced by *Vous désirez?*

Provided the context is clear, that is that the pupils are aware of the language area they are guessing, then they do not have to understand every word of the contextualising phrase in this initial stage. However, hearing something many times will signal to them that this is obviously an important piece of language which needs to be worked out. In the end, they will need to be able to ask the question themselves. So in the course of drilling the new vocabulary, it can be helpful if every time the teacher uses the contextualising phrase, he or she holds up a flashcard, on which is a large question mark, and states *La question est … qu'est-ce que tu apprends à l'école?* This will draw the pupils' attention even more explicitly to the question form. After a while the teacher can challenge them to work out what the question was by simply asking: *Et la question était …?*

2. Making pupils guess what the new words are

The teacher now has a number of options for making the pupils struggle to arrive at the meaning. In each case, he or she is aiming for pupils to guess what subject is meant, asking *comment dit-on* or *c'est quoi en français;* for example, *c'est quoi en français, Chemistry?* We will see how this key phrase can be taught in the examples below. The arrow indicates how the teacher's introduction can provoke the question.

- Describe the subject using plenty of mimes and cognates, that is words which are the same or nearly the same in the target language, some of which may need to be written on the board – *Ça se passe dans un laboratoire. Il y a beaucoup d'explosions.*

--------------→

C'est quoi en français, Chemistry?

(In section 6 of this chapter, we will see how the use of paraphrases like this can be extended not just to encourage pupils to guess at the meaning but eventually to develop their **own** ability to paraphrase. This is an important skill to promote if they are to find ways of explaining what they mean to a native speaker when they do not know the exact word in the target language.)

- Give clues by indicating – *ça commence avec g, c'est comme en anglais.*

———————▶

C'est quoi en français, Geography?

- Give a definition using the language targeted – *C'est ma matière préférée. J'adore ça. M. Davies est le professeur.*

———————▶

C'est quoi en français, History?

A useful feature of the *c'est quoi en francais?* question is that it also ensures comprehension since, although the target language is being used, the English 'filling' clarifies the meaning for the benefit of the whole class. However, like everything else, it will have first to be taught and practised.

3. *Teaching pupils how to ask* c'est quoi en français, Chemistry?

On the first occasion that it is planned to exploit this phrase, when a pupil asks *how do you say Chemistry in French?*, the teacher produces a visual, for example the French flag, repeating the phrase *c'est quoi en français, Chemistry?* The phrase is then drilled intensively on a whole-class basis, taking the pressure off the individual who made the initial suggestion. This drilling can take the usual form of repetition, with the teacher showing each of the symbols on the OHT and the pupils simply having to say the phrase again but replacing Chemistry with History, Geography, etc. Some further principles for such drilling will be provided towards the end of this section. Those interested in varying such routines, however, may like to consider the slightly more adventurous way of doing it suggested below.

Depending on the class, the drilling can take place on the basis of an American football team chant:

- the class is required to stand and place hands on knees in a semi-crouching position;

- the word *c'est* is said whilst each pupil hits their hands on their legs once;

- the same process is repeated by adding *quoi* thus giving two slaps on the legs corresponding to *c'est* and *quoi*;

- the class has to scratch their heads as they say *en français*;

- as the last word is said, *Chemistry*, pupils say it as loudly as they can whilst jumping full stretch into the air;

- once the class has got the idea of this, it can be taken one step further. The class is split into two halves facing each other and the procedure is repeated several times with a competition to see which side of the class can say *Chemistry* the loudest when they jump into the air. As we shall see in chapter 5, this can eventually be developed to promote the use of the phrase *Nous étions plus forts que vous!* The whole process can then be translated into pair work in which pupils argue about who was the loudest using the phrase *J'étais plus fort(e) que toi!*

A slightly less noisy alternative is to do the routine but with pupils having to say *Chemistry* very quietly/slowly/fast!

Having drilled the phrases intensively, the teacher can now return to the pupil who made the original suggestion and see if they can ask their original question using the visual support provided. It is likely that whatever routine is adopted, it will have to be repeated during several lessons until the phrase becomes an automatic part of classroom interaction.

Similarly, if a pupil finds they cannot answer a teacher's or another pupil's question a very helpful strategy is for them to say *Je ne sais pas* and then to nominate someone to help them: *Shirley/James, tu peux m'aider?* This means that every pupil has something to say whether or not they know the answer. It also begins to develop those communication strategies Dörnyei referred to in extract 9 of chapter 1.

> • Using the example of *c'est quoi en français*, can you think of a way that you could drill *je ne sais pas; tu peux m'aider?*

4. Guessing the right answer

Once a pupil has asked *c'est quoi en français, Chemistry?,* the teacher can of course supply the word and move directly into the activities for whole-class practice described in section 2.

But if the teacher is ready to be a little more ambitious, he or she can also prolong the guessing process by presenting carefully-selected alternatives from which the pupils choose the appropriate answer. Various strategies can be employed for the selection of the alternative, depending on the level of challenge required:

–   the word to be guessed is contrasted with words the pupils have never encountered before, but which are cognates or near cognates: *cravate, crème, chimie?*

–   already-known words can be contrasted with the one being guessed, the words being taken from the topic area under discussion: *mathématiques, chimie, géographie?*

–   the same process, except that the words are taken from other topic areas.

When employing alternatives, one has to be careful to vary which of the three alternatives actually represent the answer. There is a natural tendency to gravitate towards making it the third or the first of the options! An example of classroom interaction in German resulting from guessing the word could be:

P. Wie heißt Geography auf Deutsch?	P. What's Geography in German?
T. Wer weiß? Wer hat eine Idee?	T. Who knows? Has anyone any ideas?
Niemand? Also! Was meint ihr? Ist es:	Nobody? Okay! What do you think? Is it:
a Biologie	a Biology
b Erdkunde	b Geography
c Sport	c Sport
T. Was meint ihr? Habt ihr eine Idee?	T. What do you think? Any ideas?

At this point one can get the class to vote on what they think the right answer is. This could be done by a whole-class show of hands on the following basis:

T. Wer meint, 'a'? Wer meint 'b'?	T. Who thinks it's 'a'? Who thinks it's 'b'?
Wer meint 'c'?	Who thinks 'c'?

The answer can then be given but just by using the letter prefacing the appropriate alternatives. So the class is challenged to remember what the word was that was linked to the letter. This would then promote the following language:

T. Also, es war 'b'? Was war 'b'?	T. So. It was 'b'. What was 'b'? Can anyone
Wer kann sich daran erinnern?	remember?

If the class is on the ball, then they can retain the different possible answers and say the word they thought it was. Within this context we shall see, in chapter 5, how it is possible to start to gradually build up the use of more complex phrases such as:

Ich meine, es ist _____.	I think it's _____.
Ich glaube, es ist _____.	I believe it's _____.
Ich würde sagen, es ist _____.	I'd say it's _____.
Es ist _____, meine ich.	It's _____, I think.
Es ist _____, glaube ich.	It's _____, I believe.
Es ist _____, würde ich sagen.	It's _____, I'd say.

Providing pupils with the means to ask *c'est quoi en français ...?* means that they can be given some limited opportunities, even in the presentation phase, to choose what they want to learn. If the topic is *free time*, for example, they can ask *c'est quoi en français collecting posters/helping Dad with his motorbike*, etc.

For now, let us assume that the meaning of all the symbols on the OHT has been established. Pupils still need:

a   to get their tongues round the new sounds;
b   to remember which word is which;
c   to learn to spell them.

Traditionally, we use questioning techniques and worksheets for this process. How can the same aims be accomplished but in a way where conveying real meanings is at the forefront and pupils are encouraged to use the language spontaneously to get things done in the same way as they did when learning their first language?

Section 2: Initial whole-class practice with the teacher

The usual drills involve pointing at a symbol and asking questions that move from:

- the closed type of question: *c'est l'histoire, oui ou non?*
- to supplying alternatives: *c'est l'histoire ou l'anglais?*
- to the open-ended: *c'est quoi en français?*

To avoid pupil embarrassment in case they struggle, we tend to carefully scaffold the interaction. Johnstone, however, (1989, p25) notes that these kinds of *problem-reducing strategies* often result in the pupils hardly producing any language at all:

Et le meilleur programme pour toi, c'était …?
Eastenders.
Bon alors … Eastenders … Tu aimes ça, Paul?

Any of the following strategies can be grafted on to provide more meaningful whole-class practice of the new language and to include, even in this practice phase, all kinds of interaction language which is reusable in many contexts. The examples below give the language for an immediate reaction, such as *I don't understand* or the language needed to say how the teacher can help, like *please focus the OHP* or *please say it again*; examples, therefore, of strategic competence. All of these would need to be practised with visual support just like *c'est quoi en français …?*

1 Bring into focus on the OHT

Bring a symbol into focus very slowly on the OHP. Language generated by this activity could be:

C'est trop flou
Ce n'est pas clair
Ce n'est pas au point

2 Gradually pull out OHTs of the symbols from a picture of a mouth (for the topic food) or a school bag (for the topic school subjects)

Encore un peu

must be said before the teacher reacts and reveals more of the symbol.

*3 Conveyor belt (as illustrated in TV's **Generation Game**) with pictures of objects from a topic (clothes, food, drinks, toys, etc) on a strip of acetate pulled across the OHT screen*

This memory game can be done slowly or fast. Pupils can work in teams to remember as many words as possible and can control the teacher's speed of presentation by use of the appropriate language:

Encore une fois

Moins vite

Plus lentement

Reculez, s'il vous plaît

Avancez, s'il vous plaît

Visual support for this language, such as a picture of a tortoise with *plus lentement* written underneath, can be used to support pupils initially.

Plus lentement!

As pupils make their first attempts at saying the word, the teacher is careful to use expressions such as *bonne prononciation*, that he or she intends pupils to produce themselves in pair work at a later stage.

Section 3: Practising the new language – moving from whole-class to pair work practice

Possibly the greatest potential for the next activities is the fact that they all make challenging and highly motivating pair work activities. Here the basic principle is that of a teacher clone technique. In other words, the teacher first models and practises the activity on a whole-class basis and then passes it over to the pupils to do in pairs. So they are virtually teaching each other – getting lots more practice than if they were waiting to answer the teacher's question and having at least some choice about what to say and when. A totally teacher-centred classroom can never be a fully interactive classroom and opportunities for pupils to have some control over their learning has to be built in from the earliest stages. Page (1992) provides very valuable case studies of teachers working towards promoting greater independence.

It goes without saying that careful attention has to be paid to introducing the language of interaction gradually and providing plenty of examples with the whole class before moving into pair work. In that respect, you will notice that the interaction language in many of the examples below is similar. This ensures that although the teacher may choose different activities each lesson, pupils will still get plenty of practice of the same expressions. In chapter 5, we will explore how each of these initial 'easier' expressions can be developed into more grammatically complex alternatives. Here, we offer just one example of such potential development in the first activity.

A. Learning the sounds of the new words

1 Lip read what the teacher is saying

The teacher silently mouths a word for a school subject and pupils must guess what he or she is saying. This encourages an awareness of different mouth/lip shapes in the target language and can help accurate pronunciation. Once pupils have understood the activity, they do it in pairs.

In the next step, the teacher deliberately mouths the word too fast or unclearly. The class has to use its strategic competence with phrases that can gradually be built up in terms of complexity beginning with:

Encore une fois, s'il vous plaît!
Plus lentement, s'il vous plaît!

and much later developing into:

Vous pourriez dire ça encore une fois?
Vous pourriez dire ça plus lentement?
Ce n'était pas assez clair.

After modelling this activity several times, it can then be handed over to the pupils.

Pair work – partner A: *Qu'est-ce que tu apprends à l'école?* then mouths the word *Biologie*. Partner B tries to guess what it is, asking, if puzzled, *Je ne sais pas* and adding:

Encore une fois, s'il te plaît!
Plus lentement, s'il te plaît!

2 Mime the word

The teacher mimes drawing a picture – pupils guess – *le dessin*.

Again, this can be made more complex, if he or she mimes it too fast or very badly!

Pair work – *plus lentement, trop vite, pas clair.*

3 Hum a word/phrase

This can prompt the same language as in example 2. Humming is particularly useful to illustrate the musicality both of single words and, more significantly, words in combination: *je déteste la géographie*. It presents a model of appropriate, if somewhat exaggerated, intonation.

To add more language the teacher can ask:

Vous avez deviné?

This provides the class not only with a good game to play with the teacher and each other but begins to build up the language of encouraging the teacher or the rest of the class to guess.

Pair work – *encore une fois, pas clair, trop vite, devine.*

4 Give the first syllable and beat out the next syllables on the table – for example, géographie, mathémathiques.

Like the humming, rhythm can help pronunciation and memorisation.

Pair work – *encore une fois, pas clair, trop vite.*

5 Slow reveal and quick flash

Have the symbol of a subject already covered up on the OHT and then reveal it slowly. Alternatively a piece of paper can be quickly removed from and then replaced over the symbol, flashing an image very briefly onto the screen. The same procedure can also take place with a flashcard, provoking:

Encore une fois, s'il vous plaît!
Plus lentement, s'il vous plaît!

Pair work – if pupils have a worksheet or a page from the textbook between them with a set of symbols on it, they can 'quick flash' in pairs. They can choose to give their partner easy words or harder ones.

Whilst these activities may help pupils to **memorise the sounds and meanings** of the words, they will also need support in remembering how to **write** them. Again, however, pupils can be made to struggle to convey meaning both to the teacher and to each other and similar activities can be used, thus reinforcing the interaction language.

B. Learning the written word

6 Draw the word in the air, scribble the word quickly on the board/OHT

As with the activities above, the utilisation of a technique like this forces the class to use phrases such as:

Encore une fois!
Plus lentement !
Je crois que c'est …

Pair work – pupils write words in the air or rapidly in their books.

7 Put word out-of-focus on the OHP

This can result in a very effective guessing game where all the pupils can make a suggestion as to what the fuzzy words might represent.

Language designed to ask the teacher to focus the image can be:

Ce n'est pas clair.
Mais, non. Pas comme ça!

And the language of conjecture can first be modelled by the teacher, then used by the pupils:

C'est la géographie … (with rising intonation) …?
Moi, je crois que c'est la géographie …

Pair work – pupils write word faintly in pencil or just an outline of dots.

8 Display just the top or bottom of the word

Use a piece of paper to shade off the appropriate parts of the word. If you are feeling more adventurous, then cut the word in half with the missing bit hidden somewhere near at hand so that it can be rejoined with the top/bottom after the word has been guessed.

Géographie

Language generated by this could be:

C'est difficile!
Encore un peu!
Plus haut/bas!
Je crois que c'est …

Pair work – pupils write a word in the back of their books without their partner seeing and use a piece of paper to cover up the top or bottom half of it.

9 Put a word, written on a piece of OHP transparency, on the OHP screen upside down

Pupil–teacher interaction here could include:

C'est bon comme ça ou ce n'est pas bon comme ça?
Ça va ou ça ne va pas?

The class reply:

Ce n'est pas bon comme ça or *Ça ne va pas*

or even, once it has been modelled,

Mettez-le à l'endroit.

Then, in response, the teacher puts the piece of OHP transparency as a mirror image, and asks:

Maintenant/alors, c'est bon comme ça?

Pupils respond accordingly until the teacher shows the word correctly.

Pair work – pupils write a word in the back of their books but show it to each other upside down.

10 Start to write the word slowly on the board/OHT ...

... whilst giving hints as to what it could sound like, resemble, etc (*c'est comme en anglais* or *ça se passe dans un laboratoire*) . The language the teacher uses here can help them later to give their own definitions (see section 6 on teacher use of paraphrase). The activity is also very productive in terms of raising awareness of the likely letter combinations within words in the new language. Classes can be encouraged to guess as soon as possible. If the guess is correct, then they can obtain a point for their team. Language generated by this activity could include:

Encore un peu plus!
Je crois que c'est ...

Pair work – partner A writes two letters of a word for their partner to guess and copy down. Partner B asks, if unclear, for more letters to be written.

11 Feed a written word (colour coded perhaps to establish gender) slowly from the edge of the OHP onto the screen

This can be used as a prediction activity with simple questions modelled by the teacher, such as:

Et après?

Et maintenant?

Un E, ou un A?, etc.

Enfin, c'est ...? (teacher makes an incorrect suggestion which pupils can contradict vociferously!)

If the teacher stops after the first two or three letters, it is quite unnerving and pupils do not quite know how to react. Language can give them a way out and push them to express their feelings.

Alternatively one can start with the end of the word. After a while, the class can be asked whether they want to start with the end or the beginning. As with example 10, this activity is particularly good for raising awareness of letter combinations within words. If the class wants to see more of the word, then they have to interact with the teacher. Further language generated by this activity could be:

Ce n'est pas clair!

A gauche/droite!

Encore un peu!

Je crois que c'est ...

Pair work – whilst pupils in pairs cannot have access to the OHP, they can write the word in their books, or find one in their textbook and reveal it letter by letter, or start from different ends of the word.

12 Show a word with letters missing or covered up by different-sized coins/pieces of paper on the screen. Try to group them in patterns like:

b*o*o*<u>ie</u>	a*g*<u>ais</u>
g*o*r*p*<u>ie</u>	*r*n*<u>ais</u>

This is another way to focus on combinations of letters and correct spelling. It can also help pupils see similarities and differences between the way the word is pronounced and how it is spelled; for example, that the final *s* in words like *anglais* is not pronounced. In section 4, we will offer some further ideas for teaching the relationship between the written and the spoken form.

Pair work – pupils write/cover parts of words and their partner uses expressions like *enlève/bouge la pièce à gauche/droite, je crois que c'est un ...* (name of letter).

13 Put word on OHP screen letter by letter. After two or three letters turn off the projector

Guessing the next letter or the whole word can provide a useful focus for accurate spelling and an awareness of combinations of letters in the new language. The language here could include:

Rallumez/continuez

as well as:

Quelles lettres avez-vous vues?

Pair work – pupils write a word in their books letter by letter and then stop and their partner uses expressions like *continue*.

14 Upside-down feed onto the OHT

This is the same process as above, except that this time the word is upside-down. This just raises the level of challenge for the pupils.

15 Quick dash across the OHP

Pull a word very quickly across the projector so that it is difficult to see. The class has to interact with the teacher in order to slow down this process. Language generated by this activity could be:

Pas si vite!
Trop vite!
Plus lentement!

Pair work – partner A, without the partner seeing, writes a word on a piece of paper and quickly shows it. Partner B tries to guess what it is.

16 Give clues as to the first/last letter

Teacher says *ça commence/finit par ...* and pupils must guess, using language like *je crois que c'est ...*

Pair work – pupil A gives first/last letter. Pupil B must guess.

In this section, we have offered sixteen suggestions for meaningful language use but pupils can be invited to invent more. They are often far more imaginative at devising games than we are and appreciate the opportunity to take some control over the activities they do.

- Most of the examples above are in French. Whilst the same basic teaching principles apply across all the languages we teach, sometimes the grammar of a language presents particular problems. Try translating the following into German/Spanish to have a sense of the level of difficulty.
- Too fast!
- Slower, please.
- Lower!
- More, please!
- Again, please.
- Up/down a bit!
- Not like that!

You may also be wondering how to help pupils move from the formal polite form (*vous*) with the teacher to the more familiar form appropriate with their partner (*tu*). Since this distinction does not exist in modern English, many pupils find it difficult. One activity that some teachers use to practise the difference is to place a paper crown (from a Christmas cracker, for example) on their or their pupil's heads to elicit the more formal form. What other activities do you use?

Section 4: Tackling pronunciation

We have referred a number of times to the need to help pupils with their pronunciation. Although cognates are extremely useful in reading a text, they do cause pronunciation problems, as pupils tend to assume that they can say them as they would in English. They can also cause problems in listening comprehension, as pupils may fail to recognise them. The relationship between the spoken and the written word in French in particular raises a range of difficulties. Consider for example the French pronunciation of *tion* in *nation, natation*. Or the fact that the final consonant is not sounded (*port, grand, petit*) unless there is an *e* following it (*porte, grande, petite*). Again, we can actively involve pupils in tackling such problems, this time by encouraging them to spot patterns for themselves.

1 put up a list of cognates on OHT, for example, *port, grand, table, cinema, nation, theatre*;
2 class reads them out in English;
3 teacher adds overlay to put in accents: *théâtre*;
4 teacher reads out French words;
5 then one pupil reads out *port* and the teacher reads out the French *port*. The class has to decide what the difference is;
6 a set of rules is thus built up, e.g. non-pronunciation of final consonant;
7 teacher produces a few more words (*chat, soupe*) and gets class to pronounce them using the rules that they have worked out;
8 after further discovery of other rules (nasals for example, *th*, *r*, or unpronounced plural *s*) the teacher can pronounce a few English words with a French accent. Place names are good: Bournemouth, Southampton, for example, or the names of football

teams or pop groups. Individual pupils choose their own words and do the same while the rest of the class have to guess what the English word is. The game can then be carried out in pairs;

9   teacher then reads whole sentences in French, making some deliberate errors. Pupils can issue instructions like *arrêtez, erreur!* Finally, pupils in teams can tackle reading the sentences, with the opposing team invited to award points and comment: *bonne prononciation.*

Of course, pupils will need to be reminded of the rules but at least in this way pupils can get some idea of consistency in French pronunciation, instead of having to tackle each new word separately as it comes up.

Section 5: Revising topics

The next activities are appropriate for revising all the language associated with a topic, or even several topics prior to an end-of-unit test. They also offer the possibility of different ways of consolidating the interaction language recently met. Since the examples so far have been in French, they will now be indicated in German.

1   Keyhole techniques

For this activity cut a small keyhole in a piece of paper. The keyhole is then moved across a number of words on the OHT screen. How the keyhole is moved can be directed by the class with such phrases as:

Nach oben!	Up!
Nach unten!	Down!
Nach rechts!	Right!
Nach links!	Left!

Pair work – partner A writes eight words, taken from recent topics, on an A4 piece of paper. He or she has a keyhole cutout and moves it as directed by his or her partner. The game is to guess the eight words in the shortest time possible.

2   Hangman

This is quite a time-consuming approach; however, it is an effective way of puzzling out a complicated word. The language of interaction associated with this activity can be very useful within the context of looking at spellings and endings. The game can be shortened by providing from the word go the first and last letter of the word. Initially this is quite a good strategy since it promotes the use of some very useful metalanguage (the language we use to talk about language!), for example: *Es beginnt mit ... /es endet mit ... /It begins with ... /it ends with ...*

Classes can be encouraged to guess as soon as possible what they think the word is. This is particularly good if done on a teacher versus class basis. In such a scenario, a few extra elements of the gallows can be added, if the guess is wrong. Below is an example of the interaction that can arise from such an activity.

T. *Also, ich möchte Vorschläge, bitte. Könnt ihr bitte einige Buchstaben geben?*

T. Okay, I would like some suggestions, please. Can you give me a few letters?

P. *Ich möchte ein ‚P'.*

P. I would like a 'P', please.

T. *Es tut mir furchtbar leid, es gibt kein ‚P'. Das ist aber toll, weil ich einen Punkt gekriegt habe! Okay, andere Buchstaben, bitte!*

T. I'm terribly sorry but there isn't a 'P'. But that's great because I've got a point! Okay, another letter, please!

P. *Ich möchte ein ‚F'.*

P. I'd like an 'F'.

T. *Das ist leider richtig.*

T. Unfortunately, that's right.

P. *Ich möchte ein ‚O'.*

P. I'd like an 'O'.

T: *Es tut mir furchtbar Leid. Es gibt leider kein ‚O'.*

T. I'm terribly sorry. There is no 'O', unfortunately.

3 Give us a clue

In this game, the teacher thinks of a word and gives clues as to what it is by suggesting whether it is a pet, food, drink, hobby, what colour it is and so on. He or she can also suggest what the first syllable sounds like, if it is a long or a short word, etc. This activity is more sophisticated than the other examples but again is particularly effective in helping pupils to begin to talk about the language itself and for the production of paraphrases/circumlocution (*it's like a …*). Furthermore, it is something which the whole class can be engaged in in an almost pantomime-type fashion.

Es ist ein Name! — It's a name!

Es ist ein kleines Wort! — It's a small word!

Erste Silbe! — First syllable!

Zweite Silbe! — Second syllable!

Dritte Silbe! — Third syllable!

Es klingt wie _____. — It sounds like _____.

Man kann es trinken/essen. — You can drink/eat it.

Es ist: — It's:

süß/sauer — sweet/sour

gesund/ungesund — healthy/unhealthy

teuer/billig — expensive/cheap

Also, es ist _____! — Okay, it's _____!

Ich glaube/meine es ist _____! — I believe/think it's _____!

Pair work – partner A chooses a word from a recent topic like food/animals/clothes and says:

Man kann es essen	You can eat it
Es ist gesund	It is healthy
Es ist grün	It is green

Partner B guesses, saying:

Es ist ein Apfel, meine ich	It's an apple, I reckon
Es ist ein … , glaube ich	It's a … , I think

Section 6: Teaching pupils to paraphrase

To prepare pupils for this kind of pair work, the teacher will first have needed to provide plenty of practice in how to paraphrase. In the example below, we will see how the teacher can model it even in the **presentation** stage, by supplying definitions of the word to be guessed:

- using analogies, i.e. saying something is like something;
- using opposites, i.e. saying something is not X but Y;
- using synonyms, e.g. *It is terrible, awful, dreadful*;
- using delayers so as to teach the class the 'fillers' or stalling strategies that give them time to think, e.g. *well … , let me see;*
- giving lots of attention to the effective use of markers in the sentence which indicate that some fresh information is about to appear, e.g. *and, but, what is more*, etc.
- slowing down slightly from one's normal speed of speaking and using exaggerated intonation and emphasis to emphasise that something important is coming up;
- recycling key messages and phrases in a way that allows the class time to process meaning more effectively;
- using cognates and near cognates.

In this example, the pupils are learning how to say what they enjoy eating, responding to the contextualising question: *Was isst du gern? (What do you like eating?)*. The answer is not given directly, but the food is described through paraphrase in the target language. As with all paraphrase, the word or phrase being described becomes clearer as the paraphrase progresses.

Was isst du gern? *Das ist die Frage. Ja?*	What do you like eating? That's the question, okay?	Teacher holds up flash card with question mark on. This signals that the contextualising phrase is being used.
Also, was kann man sagen …? *Moment mal …*	So, what can I say ..? Just a moment …	Body language conveys the sense that you are thinking. Here we have the start of a delayer strand.

Ach ja! Es ist fantastisch, es ist wunderbar, es ist toll und es ist **so** *lecker! Lecker, ja? Eis, zum Beispiel, ist lecker, ja? Schokoladeneis, Vanilleeis und so weiter, ja? Lecker. Es schmeckt* **mir** *sehr sehr gut.*	Well, it's fantastic, it's wonderful, it's **so** delicious! Delicious, okay? Ice-cream, for example, is delicious, okay? Chocolate ice-cream, vanilla ice-cream, etc. okay? Delicious. I really love it!	Body language is used to convey extra meaning for the adjectives with special emphasis on the word *delicious*, e.g. rub tummy, smack lips, etc. The cognates modelled here will later be used by the pupils, as will *Es schmeckt* **mir** *sehr gut.*
Also, es ist lecker. U̴ND! Und! Man kann es essen, ja? Essen.	So, it's delicious. AND! And! You can eat it, okay? Eat.	Do a mime for eating. Particular emphasis is given to conjunction *und.*
Also. Was kann man noch sagen? Moment mal! Ach ja! Es ist braun. Ein Bär ist braun, meine Haare sind braun. Und vielleicht ein bisschen grau, weil ich so alt bin. Ja? Also, es ist braun, ja? Braun **und,** **und oder** *weiß. Schnee ist weiß. Die Tafel ist weiß. Ja? Alles klar?*	So. What else can I say? Just a moment! Oh yes! It's brown. A bear is brown, my hair is brown. And perhaps a little grey because I'm so old. Okay? So it's brown, okay? Brown *and, and or* white. Snow is white. The board is white. Okay? Alright?	Delayers are used again. Pointing gets across the colours, as well as paraphrase. *Und* continues to be stressed and a gesture and emphasis is brought in for *oder.*
Also es ist fantastisch, wunderbar und **so** *lecker. Man kann es essen* **und** *es ist braun oder weiß.*	So, it's fantastic and wonderful and **so** delicious. You can eat it **and** it's brown or white.	Here there is a slight recap with the class being challenged to put in key words. These would be *lecker, essen, braun* and *weiß.*
Und *es ist normalerweise sehr süß. Also, nicht sauer, nicht bitter. Süß! Zucker ist, zum Beispiel, süß. Tate and Lyle machen Zucker, ja? Zucker. Man trinkt eine Tasse Tee, ja? Mit Zucker.*	**And** it is usually very sweet. Not sour, not bitter. Sweet! Sugar, for example, is sweet. Tate and Lyle make sugar. Okay? Sugar. You drink a cup of tea, okay? With sugar.	The negative strand which is very useful in the field of grammar correction is being stressed.
Und was noch? Was kann man noch sagen? Moment mal! Ach ja! Es hat viel Milch. Milch, ja? Milch kommt von einer Kuh, ja? Und eine Kuh macht ‚muh‘! Milch kann man auch auf Cornflakes tun oder in eine Tasse Tee tun. Und so weiter und so fort, ja? Milch.	What else? What else can I say? Just a moment! Oh yes! It's got a lot of milk in it. Milk, okay? Milk comes from a cow, okay? And a cow says 'moo!'. You can put milk on your cornflakes or in a cup of tea, etc., okay? Milk.	The delayer strand is repeated. Pupils are invited to draw on their world knowledge. In addition there is quite a lot of stress on the emerging use of *man kann.*
Was noch? Was kann man noch sagen? Moment mal! Also ja! Leider! Und das ist eine Katastrophe. Leider hat es ganz, ganz viele…	What else? What else can I say? Just a moment! Oh yes! Unfortunately. And that's a real catastrophe. Unfortunately it's got lots and lots …	Here is some future content with the use of the word *leider.* There is also lots of stress in this next section on the use of cognates and pauses to get across meaning.

... Hunderte aber Hunderte von ... ... Kalorien!	... hundreds and hundreds of ... ... calories!	
Es ist eine Kalorienbombe!	It is packed full of calories!	
Okay. Wer ist hier sehr intelligent? Was könnte es sein? Habt ihr Ideen? Vorschläge? Was meint ihr?	Okay. Who is very intelligent? What could it be? Any ideas? Suggestions? What do you reckon?	Here we have a near cognate, i.e. *Ideen* which is leading us, hopefully, into an understanding of *Vorschläge.*
Also, Peter! Was meinst du? Was isst du gern?	Okay, Peter! What do you reckon? What do you like eating?	Here the contextualising question is being used again, as well as one of the most important questions in German language learning, *Was meinst du?* Finally pupils put up hands and ask *Wie heißt ... chocolate ... auf Deutsch?*

Table 2.2. Teacher use of paraphrase

As time progresses, we should aim for less redundancy and support via mimes, and for more reliance on the power of the words alone; the *context-reduced* situation described by Cummins in extract 7 of chapter 1. Unless our support is gradually withdrawn, pupils may never learn to infer meaning by listening to clues from the language itself. We need to move towards a situation where they are not reliant on the teacher (or eventually the native speaker) performing a song and dance act!

As pupils become familiar with key expressions, the teacher can hand over the activity to them, to play in pairs as a guessing game. The OHT in Table 2.3 may be necessary to support them, along with a choice of fillers/delayers like:

Also,

Also, na ja ...

Also, na ja, Moment mal

Was noch?

Was kann ich sagen?

A. Also, was kann man sagen? Moment mal!	A. So, what can I say? Just a moment!
Ja, man kann es essen/trinken.	Well, you can eat/drink it.
Man kann es heiß/kalt essen/trinken.	You can eat/drink it hot/cold.
Es ist: schwarz/weiß/braun/blau/grün/rot.	It's: black/white/brown/blue/green/red.
Es ist sehr/ziemlich:	It's very/quite:
süß/sauer,	sweet/sour,
gesund/ungesund,	healthy/unhealthy,
teuer/billig,	expensive/cheap,
heiß/kalt,	hot/cold,
lecker/ekelhaft,	delicious/disgusting,
nass/trocken.	wet/dry.
Man kann es mit Milch/ohne Milch trinken.	You can drink it with/without milk.
Man kann es mit Sahne/ohne Sahne essen.	You can eat it with/without cream.
Es kommt von der Kuh.	It comes from a cow.
Es kommt aus Frankreich/Italien/Indien/	It comes from France/Italy/India/
China/Brasilien/Holland/England …	China/Brazil /Holland/England …
Es sprudelt/sprudelt nicht.	It's fizzy/not fizzy.
Es ist eine/keine Kalorienbombe!	It's got loads of/a few calories.
B. Also, ich glaube das ist ____.	B. Well, I think it's ____.
Wie heißt ____ auf Deutsch?	What's the German for ____?

Table 2.3. OHT to support pupil use of paraphrase

- If you are wondering why on earth one should go through such antics in order to get across the meaning of a word, then it might be useful to refer back to extracts 8 and 9 of chapter 1; to Canale's definition of strategic competence and to the communication strategies listed by Dörnyei. It is usually the case when abroad that you have to struggle to convey meaning. After all, a native speaker is not going to be able to give you a translation of all the words you do not know. So, here you would be teaching your class some useful strategies for coping on their own. We would also like to think that the genuine challenge in these games can make the lesson more interesting.

Section 7: Some key principles of presenting and practising new language

What are the principles behind the examples we have suggested in sections 1–6?

- Look back to Skehan's summary of research into different learning styles in extract 12 of chapter 1. How does it relate to the various classroom activities we have suggested for the presentation and practice stages?

If individuals each have their own preferred learning styles (visual, auditory or kinaesthetic, for example), then, in order to facilitate retention, new words and phrases need to be exploited in a way that caters for them. Multi-sensory drilling not only provides suitable memory hooks in terms of sound and meaning, but, as we shall see in chapter 5, also stresses the relevant grammatical features of the words and phrases in question.

Visual exploitation means, on the humblest level, some sort of visual support. Unfortunately it appears to be a commonly-accepted orthodoxy that pupils should not be exposed to written forms until they have mastered the pronunciation of a word. Adopting such an approach makes language learning so much more difficult for pupils whose preferred sensory style is visual. What right have we to deprive them of their most effective way of learning? Potential concerns about pronunciation problems can usually be alleviated since the new language will also be exploited though auditory activities. Even if pronunciation problems do occur, as we have seen in section 4, this can open up a discussion of sound/spelling relationships. The language arising from this process is invaluable for promoting the earliest stages of metalinguistic discussion in L2; enabling pupils to use the language to talk about the language (in this case, correct/incorrect pronunciation of a word). The use of colour coding and categorisation (e.g. placing flashcards on the board under two columns, one for masculine and one for feminine words) also provides important visual support to draw the pupils' attention to key grammatical features like genders and verb endings.

Auditory exploitation means that the phrase is stressed as memorably as possible from a sound and rhythm point of view. Linking this process to visual support will help the auditory learner to become better on the visual channel and vice-versa. In chapter 5, we will see the use of songs to support such learners, but activities like *Hum the word* will also clearly appeal to their learning style.

Kinaesthetic exploitation means that every effort is taken to link some sort of movement or action to the phrase in question. If at all possible, the affective dimension is also stressed. In fact, the more emotional heat and intensity that can be generated through the use of a phrase in a particular context, the better this is for emphasising the communicative potential of the phrase. Although this last point may not always be possible, it is easy to find some sort of appropriate mime to help with retention. There are two types of mimes: a mime for sound and a mime for meaning. If both of these can be linked, then all the better. For example, when pupils have to repeat *il pleut,* they could say it in a low voice and slowly like a heavy shower of rain (sound), while also raising their hands above their heads and lowering them to the ground, like rain falling (meaning).

> • Look again at the examples from 1–16. For each one, tick the type(s) of exploitation used.

Number	Visual	Auditory	Kinaesthetic
1			
2			
3			
4			
5			
etc			

The vital thing about the language of interaction in pair work is that very little of the language, if any at all, should be new. If there is too much new language, then the whole activity will stall. It is both a matter of grafting a small amount of new language onto a well-established stock, and also a matter of recycling in different combinations phrases which have been used elsewhere in the learning process. The last point is particularly important in fostering the pupils' ability to transfer language into other contexts, thereby encouraging them to appreciate the communicative potential of the phrases in question.

> • How would you practise the interaction expressions listed in examples 1–16? Repetition? Mime? Would you provide written support from the word go?
>
> • Once pupils were familiar with the basic expressions, how could you extend them so they were using more complex constructions like: *could you please speak more clearly/we cannot see it properly/I would say that it is a …?* In what way could this feed into their developing grammatical understanding?

Finally, let us return to our nine school subjects to see how subsequent lessons might build on the principles discussed in this chapter to enable pupils to move from just practising the new topic language to producing it for themselves in a meaningful task.

Section 8: From presentation to production – classroom experiments with student teachers

As tutors in teacher training institutions, also with limited experience of this approach to presenting language, we decided to work with our own student teachers in school. In several projects, some short, some more sustained, we set about devising classroom materials which involved secondary school pupils in this kind of activity.

The first step involved thinking of a suitable end-of-unit problem solving task around the topic of **school subjects**. It needed to have the necessary communicative ingredients of challenge, purpose and outcome. The principles behind such tasks are discussed in detail in the next two chapters along with a range of illustrations. Here we will give just one example, the **diamond ranking activity**, described in Brown and Brown's book (1996). It was originally developed by humanities teachers to promote an understanding that there are no 'right answers' and other people's views must be respected. For example, pupils must prioritise by placing in rank order the most important quality of a good parent or the most important action to be taken to protect the environment. For beginners in language learning, the task can be adapted to a more basic level. In this case, the purpose was for a class of eleven–twelve-year-old pupils, working in groups of two or three, to establish what were the most popular school subjects and to recognise and acknowledge differences in opinion. First, though, there was a pre-activity speculation task done by the whole class, who attempted to predict what the most and least favourite subjects might be. The diamond ranking activity had the names of the nine school subjects on small pieces of card, which pupils had to order in the diamond pattern, with the **favourite** subject at the top and the **least favourite** at the bottom, deciding for example, that chemistry would be number 8.

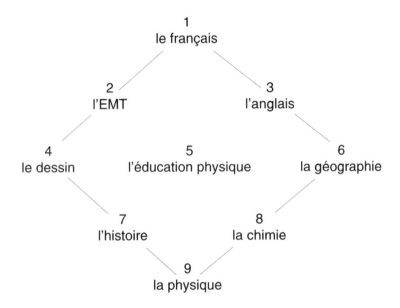

First the student teachers carried out the diamond ranking activity themselves with groups of three carrying out the activity and a fourth person – an observer – taking notes. The use of an observer meant that the language used during the process was listed and noted. It was, of course, clear that for the task to be suitable for beginning learners, considerable simplification of the language would be necessary. This was done in discussion and a final version was agreed.

- What language do you think is the bare minimum for carrying out the diamond ranking activity? You will need to consider not just the topic language (the school subjects) but also the interaction language pupils will require to make suggestions as to which card should go where, to agree and disagree with each other and so on.

- You may want to compare your key words and phrases to the list below and then to look at the list at the end of this section for some additional interaction language that the student teachers had not predicted but found was useful:

- Nine school subjects plus:

  Qui commence? Toi, moi
  Pour moi, l'anglais, c'est ma matière préférée
  Je préfère ...
  Le numéro un, c'est ...
  La géographie, c'est numéro 3 ou 4?
  L'histoire, c'est ... comme ça! (placing subject on a square)
  Non, pas comme ça!
  C'est ça
  Parfait!
  Ça y est!

A slightly different list of key expressions can be found in case study 2 in chapter 4, where Sandra Viegas describes a diamond ranking task she undertook but this time on the topic of *House and Home*.

We realised that during the presentation and practice phases of the sequence of lessons on school subjects, we would have to focus on the key interaction expressions that pupils would need for the diamond ranking activity. If we left it to the last moment, it was unlikely that pupils would be able to produce these expressions spontaneously during the task. It would therefore have to be drip-fed into preceding lessons. So we set about exploring a sequence of activities that would allow us to do this. To be reassured that it would work for other teachers, all the student groups trialled it in their classes roughly according to the description below. Some of the student teachers produced something slightly different; a positive point since they were able to bring to the task more of their own inventiveness and creativity. For their tutor, the different versions also served as a diagnostic test to see if they had understood the main principles of planning outlined below.

1 Introducing and practising the new language: contextualising the school subjects

The topic was contextualised using OHT cut-outs representing the different school subjects. During the contextualising phase the student teachers were careful to use the key language which was going to occur later on.

> • Imagine undertaking the contextualisation stage of the lesson. How could you begin to 'drip-feed' the interaction language?

Now compare your ideas with the following activities;

KEY

T = teacher
P = pupil
P1 = pupil 1
P2 = pupil 2 where both pupils work in pairs

The key words that pupils will eventually need for the diamond ranking task are in ***bold italics.***

Using OHTs to show symbols representing Maths and Geography the student teachers asked, pointing at Maths:

T. *C'est quoi **comme matière**? C'est **comme** l'anglais …*

T. *Vous avez des idées? Qu'est-ce que vous pensez?*

T. *Ça **commence** par M.* (mimes M … writes it on the board)

P. *C'est quoi en français, Maths?*

(C'est quoi en français? C'est quoi en anglais? were familiar phrases and had been used before this particular lesson.)

T. *Bien! **C'est ça.** Mathématiques.*

The school subjects were then practised using the activities 1–16 in sections 2 and 3 of this chapter, paying particular attention to language like ***parfait, c'est ça*** that would be needed later, for example:

T. (Showing blurred OHT of History….)
    *Ça **commence** par H …*

T. *C'est quoi **comme matière** …?*

P. *Je crois que c'est …*

T. ***Parfait!** Génial! **C'est ça/Non, ce n'est pas ça**. Je suis désolé …*

Partner work

P1.*C'est quoi **comme matière**?*
    *Ça **commence** par D …*

P2.*C'est …*
P1.*Parfait!*

Visual support for these phrases was shown on the board.

*C'est quoi **comme matière**?*

*Ça **commence** par ...*

C'est ...?

C'est ça! Ce n'est pas ça.

Parfait!

2   *Revision of numbers and pronunciation practice*

The nine OHTs of the school subjects were shown on the board, each of them numbered. This allowed the teachers both to revise the numbers and also model the question needed for the diamond ranking task.

T. *Les maths, c'est **numéro un ou numéro deux**?*

P. **Numéro deux.**

They then varied the questioning so that they could use the language of praise to refine pronunciation of the subjects, whilst at the same time reinforcing some of the interaction language that would be needed.

T. (feigning not having heard) *C'est quoi **numéro deux**?*

P. *Les maths.*

T. *Ah, oui. **C'est ça!** Bonne prononciation! **Numéro deux**, c'est les maths.*

They prevented interference from the written word by inviting pupils to read the words:

T. *Lisez les mots.*

T. ***Pas comme ça**. Ça se prononce ...*

T. *Bonne prononciation.*

Partner work – pairs read the words: ***Pas comme ça**, c'est ...*

Each time the phrases were modelled by the student teachers and substantially practised as a whole class activity, before they were transferred into partner work for pupil-pupil use.

By this stage pupils were able to:

1   recognise names of school subjects in oral/written form;
2   pronounce them with reasonable accuracy *with support;*
3   produce them orally *with support* and in written form;
4   spell the names of the subjects accurately;
5   produce the numbers.

3   *Introducing* **qui commence, moi, toi** *etc ...*

As pupils were now becoming familiar with words like ***commence, toi, moi**, the student teachers encouraged them to begin subsequent pair work by deciding who would start.

They went back to the numbered symbols which represented the school subjects and modelled the question again:

Numéro un, *c'est quoi?*

They then invited the pupils to ask them the questions, adding:

Qui commence? Moi/toi?

This was followed by pupils undertaking teach-and-test activities on each other;

P1 Qui commence? Moi/toi? Numéro un, *c'est quoi?*

P2 *C'est … /Je ne sais pas. C'est quoi en*
     français Geography?

P1 Bonne prononciation!/Pas comme ça.

and a competition to see who could get all nine correct in the shortest time.

4 Pupils produce 'pour moi, numéro un, c'est …; mes matières préférées sont …'

The student teachers wrote the names of four subjects on the board, parts of which were illegible or 'gapped' or fuzzy or half visible.

T. *Pour moi numéro un,* **c'est …**
     C'est aussi la matière préférée/la matière numéro un de
     Mlle … Devinez.

The class responded, guessing:

Numéro un, *c'est …*

Pair work – pupils were asked to write their own list of subjects, placing them in rank order of preference, but leaving out some letters in each word.

1   – – g – – – –

2   – – s – o – r –

3   – – – – – – a – – – – –

Pupils then went round sharing their list with other members of the class saying:

P1 **Pour moi numéro un/deux c'est …?** *Devine …*

P2 *Anglais/Je ne sais pas.*

P1 **C'est ça/** Gives clues – for example, **ça commence/finit par A …**

The teachers could spot as they eavesdropped on the oral work which pairs of pupils needed more individual help.

5 *Preparing for the diamond ranking activity*

To shift this now to the diamond ranking context, the student teachers modelled the activity on the board, moving OHTs of the subjects saying:

Pour Kenny, le numéro un c'est ...

Pour Cathy, le numéro deux c'est ...

Pupils were then invited to come up the board and use the language to report on the preferred subjects of other pupils they had interviewed.

Now that they had the language and understood the task, the class could start the activity.

Additional language

In spite of having identified in advance the key words and expressions they **thought** the pupils would need and that they would therefore attempt to use as often as possible, in the event the student teachers found that they also used other expressions. If used on many occasions pupils often pick these up and incorporate them into their own linguistic repertoire. So it is always helpful to note words or phrases which recur. Much of this language expresses either an ordering device, or turn-taking procedures or an expression of an emotional response – all personal, memorable and re-usable. Such interaction language can become the linguistic goal of many lessons and needs to be noted and developed as the learning continues. Indeed, pupils should be invited to contribute their own suggestions as to useful language the class needs to learn. Among these additional expressions were:

> d'accord/pas d'accord
> c'est difficile!
> moi aussi!
> toi aussi!
> ensuite

Conclusion

Although limited in scope, the student teachers' projects with their Year 7 classes were beginning to show, once a mind set had been established, that pupils could use more and more language with the teacher and then with each other. After a while this language became well established and occurred more and more frequently, even though its range was very modest. It did, however, need to be planned over time and always carefully modelled at the outset. It seemed that it is both possible and preferable to introduce interaction language with language learners as they **begin** their language learning experience. Leaving such an experience until later, when pupils are often more resistant to oral pair work, could be counterproductive. This leads us to our final section.

- In this new area, where teachers often have very little experience of making learners struggle to arrive at meaning, it may be worth conducting a departmental experiment. This not only has the advantage of sharing successes and failures in a non-judgemental way but also of seeing how each teacher interprets the task. Brief but regular meetings could be planned to describe and evaluate progress. A common approach also means that if pupils transfer from teacher to teacher they share similar linguistic resources. Since the approach takes time to become natural and spontaneous both for teacher and pupil, this shared experience is essential.

Section 9: Dealing with the disaffected – rewards and punishments!

Thus far we have assumed that the nature of the activities would be sufficiently meaningful to engage pupils' interest. But sometimes there may be a struggle, particularly initially, to lock pupils onto using the language. What can the teacher do, faced with a class of disaffected pupils? There are no easy answers but here are some strategies that we found useful, starting from the most basic and moving on to the more ambitious.

Starting out

The student teachers adopted a number of simple strategies to encourage pupils to use the target language.

1   Marie-Pierre Hamard, who also carried out a project on the topic of school subjects with a Year 7 class, used a number of **rewards**:

- When a pupil used an interaction statement, she would stop and say *Klasse, habt ihr gehört? Bitte wiederholt alle zusammen, denn es war wirklich prima. (Class, did you hear? Please repeat it together, as it was really good.)* Sometimes, she invited pupils to applaud and later they took this up for themselves, calling out *Applaus*, when they thought one of their peers had said something really good;

- She used stamps and stickers in their exercise books and comments in their record books. At half term she gave certificates and chocolate to reward pupils for their use of interaction language.

2   Diana Strasser made a display space for pupils to 'build' a wall. Each time she heard them using an interaction phrase, they wrote it on a *Sprechbaustein*, as in Figure 2.2, and stuck it up on the wall. She also asked pupils one lesson to fill in a self-assessment questionnaire on how much German they had spoken that lesson.

3   Emer McKenna had a chart on the wall with gold stickers for pupils who used interaction language. She also had a forfeit system. She appointed a police officer each lesson, but without the class knowing who it was. At the end of the lesson, the police officer would reveal him/herself and read out any expressions in English

he/she had heard. These were then stuck onto a 'rubbish bin' poster and the person who had said them had to find out the French equivalent and write it up.

4   Jim devised an on-going team competition in which points were awarded for good use of interaction language. Any kind of timed team game (including beat the teacher!) is likely to generate enthusiasm, as well as a great deal of interaction language. For example, in pairs, as fast as they can, pupils must count up from 1–10, say the alphabet, say the words for the flashcards on the board. An extra dimension can be added by getting them to say it according to their partner's instructions, for example, slowly, fast, in a happy way, a sad way, in a robot's voice. The criteria for awarding points always needs to be made explicit to the class and needs to become increasingly more challenging.

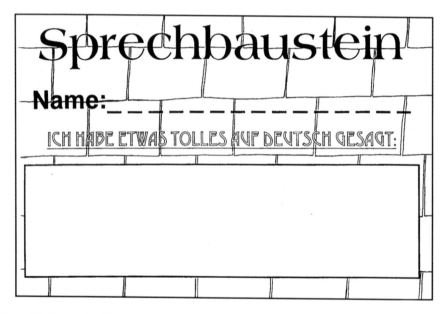

Figure 2.2. Reward wall

Moving on

1   *The* type sympa

In the diamond ranking activity, as a way of commenting on what was happening, we invented an observer role. One pupil, chosen at random by the roll of a dice – lowest number is the observer – is a *type sympa*, someone whose function is to comment on and record what is said. This person can:

•   record words/expressions during partner work that the pupils do not seem to know very well and the teacher may need to practise further next lesson;

- ask the teacher to check vocabulary or spelling which they hear but are not sure about: *ça s'écrit comment?* for example;
- have as a focus for comment pronunciation, for example, and make remarks to individuals like *bonne prononciation* or even *encore une fois* as appropriate;
- evaluate how a group is working: *bon travail* and other comments taken from familiar phrases used by the teacher feature frequently!
- comment on the mood of individuals: *Clive est de mauvaise humeur aujourd'hui,* the relevant expressions having been learned previously from a list of 'chance cards' used to give speakers an emotional role in more conventional role plays.

2 *The forfeit system*

James Stubbs (whose work is described in more detail in chapter 5) employs a **forfeit system**. This includes:

- points being awarded to the opposing team if English is used;
- negotiation, at the start of the lesson, of the forfeit to be employed during the lesson for speaking English. The forfeit is chosen through some sort of dynamic activity on the forfeit OHT (Figure 2.3). e.g. spinning a pen or unleashing a clockwork toy and seeing where it ends up. Alternatively, pupils can vote on a forfeit for each particular occasion. The forfeit system becomes more and more complex and is added to by the class themselves.
- the implementation of a *je suis désolé(e)* routine, where pupils have to apologise for speaking English, stand for a negotiated period of time and then request to sit down.

Je dois …   **Nous devons …**

Tu dois …   **Vous devez …**

Il/Elle doit …   **Ils/Elles doivent …**

Figure 2.3. Forfeit OHT

Apart from giving pupils some control over the lesson, this forfeit routine supported by the OHT allowed the class to begin to develop their grammatical awareness to the point that, later on in their learning, the following interaction took place.

[… Matthew has just said something in English …]

T: *Ah! Matthew! Toute la classe …*	Ah! Matthew! Everyone …
Class: *Ah! Matthew! Il ne faut pas parler anglais! Pourtant, tu as parlé anglais, alors, tu dois …*	Ah! Matthew! You mustn't speak English! But you did speak English so you must …
T: *… avoir un gage, bon, OK, alors, on va regarder ici et décider […] Alors, qu'est-ce que vous pensez? Demander quelqu'un au mariage?*	… have a forfeit, good, OK, so we are going to look here and decide […] So, what do you think? Ask someone to marry him?
Class: *Oui!*	Yes!
T: *Demander quelqu'un au mariage? Mmm, alors, on va décider. Alors, il y a plusieurs autres possibilités: Tu dois conjuger 'avoir', tu dois conjuger 'être', tu dois définir un verbe ou définir un verbe à l'infinitif, ou tu dois définir un nom ou un adjectif […] ou tu peux choisir. Je te donne la possibilité de choisir, OK? Qu'est-ce que tu préfères? Un, deux, etc?*	Ask someone to marry him? Mmm, well, we will decide. Well, there are several other possibilities: 'You must conjugate 'to have', you must conjugate 'to be', you must define a verb or define a verb in the infinitive or you must define a noun or an adjective […] or you can choose. I am giving you the possibility to choose, OK? What do you prefer? One, two, etc?
Matt: *Huit.*	8.
T: *Numéro huit, oui? Bon, conjuger 'avoir', OK, alors il a choisi numéro huit, mais il faut le changer un petit peu, je pense. Alors qu'est-ce qu'on peut ajouter?*	Number 8, yes? Good, conjugate 'to have', OK, so he has chosen number eight, but we have to change it a little bit, I think. So what can we add?
P: *Danser.*	To dance.
T: *En dansant? Oui, OK. Plus? Oui?*	While dancing? Yes, OK. More? Yes?
T: *En chan …*	While sing …
Class: *En chantant.*	While singing.
T: *En chantant, très bien. En chantant et en dansant, oui?*	While singing, very good, while singing and dancing, yes?
P: *Et sur la table.*	And on the table.
T: *Sur la table? Bon, OK, alors. Tu dois conjuger 'avoir' en chantant et en dansant sur la table, d'accord?*	On the table? Good, OK, so. You must conjugate 'to have' whilst singing and dancing on the table, OK?
Class: *Oui.*	Yes.
T: *OK. Alors vous dites 'Matthew …'*	OK. So you say 'Matthew …'
Class: *Matthew, il ne faut pas parler anglais! Pourtant, tu as parlé anglais, alors, tu dois conjuger 'avoir' en dansant et en chantant sur la table. Vas-y!*	Matthew, you mustn't speak English! But you did speak English so you must conjugate 'to have' whilst dancing and singing on the table. Go on!

If you are surprised by the pupils' level of grammatical awareness, you might find it reassuring to refer to chapter 5 to see how it was gradually built up over some time.

In this chapter, we have focussed on a range of ways of making the familiar presentation and practice phases of the lesson more meaningful. Some of the ideas offered are more ambitious than others. Just as pupils have their own preferred learning styles, so we, their teachers, have activities with which we are comfortable and those which make us uneasy! Some people really enjoy doing the kind of 'song and dance act' suggested in the paraphrase routine, others dislike it. It is also true that some activities are simply not appropriate for some classes.

- Look back over the various activities suggested; which do you feel suits your teaching style or your classes best?

Useful follow-up reading

Rendall, H. (1998) Pathfinder 33: *Stimulating grammatical awareness.* London: CILT. As the title suggests, the main focus of this book is not on interaction language. Nevertheless, it contains a wealth of helpful ideas showing how to cater for the different learning styles in a class, as well as how to tackle pronunciation problems.

Skehan, P. (1998) *A cognitive approach to language learning.* Oxford: Oxford University Press. Chapter 10 explores in detail the complex research into learning styles.

James, C., Clarke, M. and Woods, A. (1999) *Developing speaking skills.* London: CILT. This describes various projects undertaken in twelve schools across Wales.

Phipps, W. (1999) Pathfinder 38: *Pair work; interaction in the modern languages classroom.* London: CILT. For a range of practical ideas grouped under stages such as *repetition and imitation, manipulation* and *productive and creative.*

3

Some ideas for guided language production

Introduction

This brief chapter acts as a bridge between the preceding and the next chapter. It aims both to offer some ideas for moving on from the activities discussed in chapter 2 and to provide the context for the classroom projects described in detail in chapter 4.

In the previous chapter, we looked at how we could make presenting and practising the language more meaningful. We saw how even within these phases of the lesson, pupils could be encouraged to use the language spontaneously and to begin to develop their strategic competence. Very often, however, this was just in the form of short bursts of pair work or simple requests to the teacher. What would be the next step forward for such pupils? If we consider progression in speaking skills, then we might look to a range of factors including longer interactions, a wider range of topics and functions and so on. Following the model of the **3Ps** (Presentation, Practice and Production), we might also expect pupils to produce the language with little or no support or intervention from the teacher. Tasks requiring production of the language however, are not identical. Rather we might see them as located on a continuum from the closed to the more open-ended; from clearly structured activities where pupils are carefully guided to those where they have much more choice about what they are going to talk about and how they are going to say it. In terms of the latter, pupils may be engaging in the kinds of negotiation and reflection described in chapter 5. Following Leni Dam's (1995) pioneering work on learner autonomy, they might even use the target language to negotiate the project they wish to undertake, how they will tackle it and to evaluate their own progress. Clearly these types of task involve the *direct participation in authentic communicative interaction* referred to in the Introduction. Yet in order to reach such independence both in language use and in language learning, it seemed to us that pupils may need to engage in tasks at the other, more limited end of the continuum. We have seen how even in the presentation and practice phases of the lesson, pupils can be involved in negotiating what language to learn and suggesting possible activities. The next step might be for them to engage in longer exchanges but within tasks which are clearly defined and structured and within topic areas that have been recently taught by the teacher. Since one of the aims of our project was to review the opportunities pupils were offered in the typical classroom situation to engage in genuinely communicative tasks, we turned to coursebooks to examine the kinds of speaking tasks pupils are regularly set.

Recent coursebooks in all the commonly taught languages include speaking activities to be performed by two (or more) learners, often referred to as pair or partner work. Their function is to encourage learners to produce for themselves language recently encountered, without constant prompts from the teacher. They frequently take the form of:

- a list of questions the pupils should ask their partner, for example, about their favourite hobbies or how they spent their holidays. Sometimes such pair work may start as a substitution exercise, where pupils first practise an exchange on the lines of *Tu aimes l'histoire? Oui, c'est intéressant/Non, c'est ennuyeux* and then use the suggested pattern to ask their partner about other school subjects;
- pictoral prompts, for example, of different items to ask for at a café;
- a **flow chart** written in the target language indicating possible responses, for example, a dialogue between a sales assistant and a customer shopping for clothes;
- prompts written in English, for example:
  – ask how much it costs to send a letter to England;
  – ask where there is a telephone;
  – say thank you and goodbye.

Whilst such activities may help pupils to rehearse the language, they rarely engender the kind of spontaneous independent speech we associated with *authentic communicative interaction*. Indeed, all too often they lack one or more of the features of communication, outlined in the PIFCO acronym in chapter 1:

Purpose: pupils are often already well aware of their friend's likes and dislikes;

Information gap: if both pupils can see written or visual prompts, then there is no information to be communicated;

Feedback: if both pupils can see the prompts, they do not have to cope with the unpredictable nature of genuine communication; to understand and choose an appropriate response to what has just been said;

Context: the setting for a conversation is ill defined; who is talking to whom and where and why? There is little discernible emotional, cultural or social role to condition the message;

Outcome: since there has been no purpose for the conversation, it is unlikely that there will be an outcome.

Michael Grenfell (1994, p56) concludes that, in the case of the post office scenario:

> *This is not so much a linguistic problem as one of imagination; not so much conveying sense as trying to make sense of what is going on in a situation highly removed from any personally known facts. Discourse between individuals is not being generated in the context of shared understandings, so much as imposed in an overly prescribed manner.*

In the case of asking a partner questions about themselves:

> *Just as in pattern practice, it is unlikely that such drilling makes any real use of the natural motivational force inherent in expressing oneself in conversation; the will to be understood at that particular point in the discourse. Again, even when such exercises are satisfactorily performed, there is real reason to doubt that much of the language will be recalled and actively used when needed in speech. Real language use is just not that tidy ... My conclusion is that yes, we learn best when we are personally involved but activities based on personalised topics are not necessarily sufficient to do this; as the former implies an investment of concern that the latter can merely mimic.*

These comments may also help us to understand pupils' responses to information gap activities. In an attempt to recreate some of the features of communication, we may look beyond the coursebook for supplementary materials, designed specifically around information or opinion gap tasks. Yet all too often, because there is no real emotional involvement or genuine cognitive challenge in such tasks, the minute the teacher's back is turned, pupils simply ask each other *wot you got?*! Why should the price of a train ticket to Paris matter to them? Why should they be provoked to use the language spontaneously? In contrast to other subject areas, nor do such tasks offer any genuine cognitive challenge; there is nothing intriguing, puzzling or new to learn, other than the language itself.

We may then look towards role play, if we define it not as the stilted, artificial exchanges on the lines of *act out a conversation at the baker's shop* but rather where it adopts some of the features associated with drama (see, for example, Hamilton and McLeod 1993). Pupils take on a defined emotional role, that of being angry, weary, happy, impatient, or a role which is culturally or socially defined (a parent, a rebellious child, a lazy shopkeeper). They will be expected to use body language – gesture, facial expression, posture, eye contact, standing near to or at a distance from someone, other contact like handshakes and so on. At more advanced levels, pupils may have to use the language to resolve a conflict: should the nuclear power station be built in the area, offering employment to many or does it create too great a health hazard? Each pupil may have an assigned role (an unemployed person, a mother with three young children, an environmental campaigner and so on). Such role plays often do engage pupils' interest and can provoke genuinely spontaneous and meaningful exchanges. The problem here, however, is that it often requires moving classroom furniture, organising props and so on and we wanted to focus on tasks that could be set up on a regular basis in the typical classroom.

This then was the challenge we set ourselves and the questions we wanted to explore:

1   How could we provide genuinely communicative tasks which moved pupils beyond short bursts of pair work, yet continued to provide them with the structure and 'scaffolding' that they needed?

2   How could we ensure that pupils would really want to perform them? How could we build on Zoltan Dörnyei's 'commandment' (extract 5) in the first chapter that we should *choose interesting topics, build on learners' interests* and *make tasks challenging* to involve everyone?

In a sense, what we were trying to do was to explore the right balance between the four quadrants of Jim Cummin's model discussed in extract 7 of chapter 1, between the linguistic and the cognitive demands of a task. How could we create tasks that were intrinsically interesting enough for pupils to want to do them, whilst at the same time ensuring that they were not impossibly difficult from the language point of view?

In the rest of this chapter, we offer some tentative ways forward for encouraging such guided production of the language, particularly with younger pupils. First however, we want to stand back and view our subject from the pupils' perspective.

Pupils' perceptions of Modern Languages in the curriculum

As language teachers, we soon realise that if we make things too difficult, many pupils promptly give up. So we have become quite sophisticated at keeping the language simple in order for pupils to experience immediate success, using the *problem-reducing strategies* referred to in chapter 2. But it is possible that in the search for simplicity, we have reduced the content of our lessons to the trivial. Consider, for example, what they are studying in other lessons.

This is what they are looking at in History ...

KS3:
- The French Revolution
- World War I
- World War II
- The Battle of Hastings
- The Holocaust
- Nuclear weapons

KS4:
- The rise of fascism
- Nazi Germany
- Nazi propaganda

And in Geography ...
- The European Union
- Two countries other than the UK – physical and human features
- Environmental issues

And in RE ...
- Abortion
- Euthanasia

And in PHSE ...
- Racism
- Sex
- Drugs
- Growing up
- Family
- Relationships
- Healthy eating
- Citizenship

Figure 3.1. A summary of the curriculum in Sunderland LEA

Yet when they enter the Modern Languages classroom, the challenge that awaits them is to find out the price of a kilo of carrots! Contrasting Modern Languages with other curriculum subjects is perhaps unfair. We have to accept that our Key Stage 3 and 4 pupils are not going to be able to discuss controversial issues in L2 with the same degree of sophistication as in L1. Nevertheless, the Sunderland list can serve as a timely reminder that we may need to review critically the content of what we teach.

Making the Modern Languages curriculum more meaningful

As Do Coyle (1999, p14) points out, both teachers and pupils are constrained by the demands of the GCSE syllabus:

> *often represented by the dominance of the textbook and where learners do not find space to speak for themselves, to use language in real communicative encounters or to stimulate responses.*

However, making the content of what we teach more meaningful does not necessarily mean a fundamental change to the syllabus. It is more a matter of adding a different slant to familiar topics.

We will explore three ways in which it can be done:

1   by saying something about themselves that really is of personal significance (rather than telling their partner, who probably comes home to tea with them three times a week, how many hamsters, brothers or sisters they have got);
2   by using the language as a vehicle for genuinely learning something new about the world they live in;
3   by engaging in tasks where the group as a whole has a problem to be solved.

In the examples below, we are not suggesting that the tasks are presented to pupils at the start of a unit of work. Rather they are an **end** task, a goal towards which they are working, that can give a sense of purpose to the tedium of practising the vocabulary and structures they will need.

You will notice that all of them require the use of interaction language, that is language over and above the topic language that is needed to make the conversations work. This is because they require pupils to genuinely negotiate with each other, rather than simply to convey information. Some suggestions for ways of teaching this language have already been made in the previous chapter, and in the next chapter we will explore further possibilities. We will look in particular at how the teacher, possibly with the help of the pupils, has to identify well in advance the interaction language needed to perform the end-of-unit task, so that he or she can drip-feed it in gradually during the preceding lessons. A brief example was given with the diamond ranking activity in chapter 2. Although here the main focus is on the nature of the tasks themselves, we will periodically stop and ask you to consider the nature of the interaction language required. The intention is that you will then be in a better position to understand the issues that the teachers in chapter 4 had to take into account.

1 Personally significant tasks: my home town

Pupils are frequently asked to describe their home town. Yet there seems little point in them telling each other how many cinemas there are in an area that they both know well. An alternative is to ask them, towards the end of the unit of work, to draw a map of their immediate locality. Instead of marking in the cinema and the post office, they can choose ten places of personal significance, as in Figure 3.2. Next lesson, pupils fold back the *Key* and must find out from each other which places they chose and why.

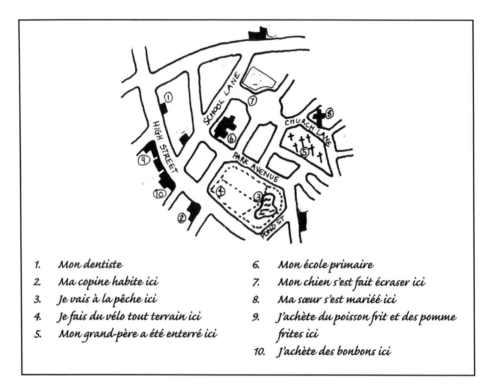

1.	*Mon dentiste*	6.	*Mon école primaire*
2.	*Ma copine habite ici*	7.	*Mon chien s'est fait écraser ici*
3.	*Je vais à la pêche ici*	8.	*Ma sœur s'est mariéé ici*
4.	*Je fais du vélo tout terrain ici*	9.	*J'achète du poisson frit et des pomme*
5.	*Mon grand-père a été enterré ici*		*frites ici*
		10.	*J'achète des bonbons ici*

Figure 3.2. My map (adapted from Hemming, J and Melor, B (1985) '*Myself*', Exeter: Arnold Wheaton.)

Much of the language used revises **topics** such as family and hobbies. More complex expressions that pupils may need, involving the passive and the perfect tense, can be treated, at this stage, as the unanalysed *chunks* that Rosamond Mitchell describes in extract 2 of chapter 1.

> • What **interaction** language would pupils need to perform this task; that is the language over and above stating the significance of each place? Try the activity with two colleagues. You draw your personal map, and one of your colleagues asks in the target language about each of the places numbered. The third person is the observer, noting down the interaction language used. What kinds of questions does your colleague ask to find out about the places? How does he or she respond when you tell him or her about the places that matter to you? Could the language you used be simplified to the level of your pupils? You may want to compare your language list with the suggestions below.

The simplest way to start the conversation is for pupils to ask each other: *numéro 1, c'est important pour toi, pourquoi?* They can either simply note their partner's replies, or we can encourage them to make simple responses such as: *comme moi, moi aussi*, or even *c'est triste ça*. We rarely teach these expressions and yet they are part and parcel of natural conversation, of discourse competence (knowing that some kind of response is appropriate) and socio-linguistic competence (adapting the response to the audience; choosing the appropriate register to use). In chapter 4, we will see from the case study of a project, carried out with pupils with Special Educational Needs, that we cannot take it for granted that pupils know how to engage in such turn-taking appropriately. Pupils' responses to each other will also involve a certain degree of **unpredictability**, since they must adapt what they say next according to what has just been said. Linguistically, however, they are no more demanding than stating *vous prenez la première rue à gauche*.

The intention is that by personalising tasks in this way, we provide pupils with some choices about what they say and a **purpose**, a wish to **communicate.** Hopefully, it can make the language real and relevant, and recognise and validate, albeit it in a limited way, their own lives, feelings and past experiences.

- Consider the familiar topic *Description of self and family members.* How interested are pupils likely to be in knowing that their partner's brother has brown hair and blue eyes?
- How could it be rendered more meaningful by adding a personal, affective dimension? In what contexts do we normally tell each other what our parents and siblings look like?

2 Tasks which involve learning something new: daily routine

The topic of *Daily Routine* is frequently covered in Key Stage 3. Yet finding out what time your partner brushes their teeth has little of intrinsic interest. Kim Brown and Margot Brown, however, show in their *Pathfinder* (1996) how the topic can be given an altogether different slant by inviting pupils to compare their daily routine to that of pupils in a Tanzanian village. Based on development education principles, the ideas and materials in their book illustrate how language learning can play an important role in the education of the child as a whole, allowing them to expand their understanding of the world around them. The target language is no longer an end in itself but rather the means of finding out about something that may genuinely interest them. At its most ambitious, such an approach may involve teaching other areas of the curriculum, History or Geography for example, through the target language. This is a growing area of interest across Europe. Here we describe some more basic starting points, drawing on suggestions from their book.

Towards the end of a unit of work on *Daily Routine* with her Year 8 pupils, Katherine Moulds, a student teacher, divided her class into two groups. Each pupil was given a slip of paper. Pupils in the first group had slips of paper with expressions describing the typical daily routine of British pupils. The slips of paper for pupils in the second group described the daily routine of a pupil in Malawi, as shown in Figure 3.3. Pupils in both groups had to read out their slips and arrange themselves in two rows according to the sequence of activities.

Je me lève à cinq heures du matin.

Je me lave dans le lac. L'eau est très froide.

J'aide maman à faire le petit déjeuner pour dix personnes. Nous mangeons du 'nsima'.

Je balaie la maison à six heures dix.

Je vais au collège à pied. J'ai trente minutes de marche.

Les cours commencent à sept heures. J'ai cinq cours le matin.

A midi je déjeune. Je mange du 'nsima' avec des haricots blancs.

Je quitte le collège à cinq heures.

A cinq heures dix je vais au marché pour acheter de la farine.

Je rentre à la maison.

J'aide maman à faire le dîner.

Je dîne à six heures. Je mange du 'nsima' avec des tomates.

Je fais mes devoirs à sept heures.

Je prépare la chambre pour moi, mes trois sœurs, mon frère et mon cousin.

Je me couche à huit heures du soir. Quelle longue journée!

Figure 3.3. Malawi daily routine

Katherine commented that the pupils engaged in the task with an enthusiasm they would not have felt, had she tried to recycle the language by further mundane tasks based on their own routine. When they got to the line *quelle longue journeé*, pupils appeared to appreciate their own relatively privileged position, without her having to make a point of it.

In both the tasks described so far, the level of linguistic challenge has been reduced by providing pupils with clear pictoral or written 'props'. This helps the language to be, in Jim Cummin's words, *context-embedded*. Nor has the level of cognitive challenge been very demanding. In the *my map* activity, pupils have already reflected on the significant places in their town, before they come to communicating with their partner. In the *Malawi* daily routine, they are simply passing on factual information that they have been given.

Similar principles apply when we move on to tasks which are a little more ambitious. The next activity involves adapting material from the Charis project (1997), in which detailed interviews are provided with a number of young people from Burkino Faso. Pupils are placed in groups; each is given a picture of one of the young people mounted on a piece of A4 paper, as in Figure 3.4. They work together to write questions round it.

Figure 3.4. Questions around a picture

Their picture is then passed on to the next group who must answer as many of the questions as they can by reading the interview with that person. Depending on the level of the class, it may be appropriate to shorten the Charis materials, as indicated below.

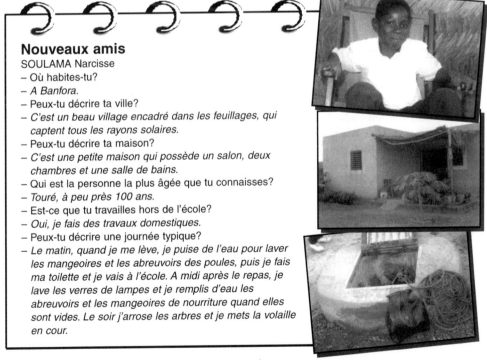

Nouveaux amis
SOULAMA Narcisse
– Où habites-tu?
– *A Banfora.*
– Peux-tu décrire ta ville?
– *C'est un beau village encadré dans les feuillages, qui captent tous les rayons solaires.*
– Peux-tu décrire ta maison?
– *C'est une petite maison qui possède un salon, deux chambres et une salle de bains.*
– Qui est la personne la plus âgée que tu connaisses?
– *Touré, à peu près 100 ans.*
– Est-ce que tu travailles hors de l'école?
– *Oui, je fais des travaux domestiques.*
– Peux-tu décrire une journée typique?
– *Le matin, quand je me lève, je puise de l'eau pour laver les mangeoires et les abreuvoirs des poules, puis je fais ma toilette et je vais à l'école. A midi après le repas, je lave les verres de lampes et je remplis d'eau les abreuvoirs et les mangeoires de nourriture quand elles sont vides. Le soir j'arrose les arbres et je mets la volaille en cour.*

Figure 3.5. Simplified extract from Charis materials[1]

We realise that some pupils may have difficulties in reading even the simplified text, although they will have met words like *l'eau, matin, laver, repas* before, albeit in a different context. Harris (1997) offers some ideas on how to teach reading strategies so that pupils are able to tackle such texts independently and with confidence. Hopefully they will want to persevere, since they have both a **purpose** and an **audience** for what they discover.

We are beginning in this example to move towards the kind of multi-skill approach, outlined by Rosamond Mitchell in extract 14, chapter 1. We will find further examples of how the other skills can support the development of communicative interaction in chapter 4.

> • How does the material for these tasks on daily routine differ from the portrayal in the media of the countries of Francophone Africa either as tropical sun havens or underdeveloped and impoverished countries?
>
> • In what way are the activities richer in terms of content than the usual GCSE topics? How could the use of such material enable Modern Languages to make a worthwhile contribution to other areas of the curriculum, as suggested by Do Coyle in extract 6 of chapter 1?

Whilst the example here was *Daily Routine*, topics like *House and Home*, *Food* and *Weather* also lend themselves very readily to such an approach. Teachers of Spanish may wish to draw on examples from South America, Mexico, etc.

3 Structured problem-solving tasks: house and home

In the adaptation of the Charis project, pupils were not only using the language to learn something new, they were also presented with a problem-solving task. In these types of task, there is no information that one person has and the other lacks. Rather the group as a whole must use information that they can all see to solve a problem. For older pupils, this might involve a task centred around the kind of content rich material we saw in the Charis materials. Initially, however, it may need to be based on some fairly straightforward factual information, using familiar language.

> With two colleagues, try out the task *Noisy Neighbours* in Figure 3.6. In this task, you are responsible for allocating tenants to a new block of flats. You should cut up the sheet showing the tenants and then try to place each of them on the most appropriate flat. You should also try to allocate a flat to your partner's family and your own.
>
> • What age group could you use this task with? As competent users of the target language, we tend to perform tasks to a high level. The disadvantage of this is that we then assume it is too hard for our pupils. What is the *bare minimum* of both topic and interaction language that might be necessary to practise with the class before the task is attempted?
>
> • What would be the advantages/disadvantages of presenting the task in the form of a worksheet, rather than with cut-up cards?

- How does this relate to the discussion of different learning styles (visual, auditory and kinaesthetic) in chapter 2?
- How does it relate to the level of challenge the task presents?
• How does the task match up to the principles of communicative language teaching (**purpose, outcome,** etc) discussed in chapter 1?

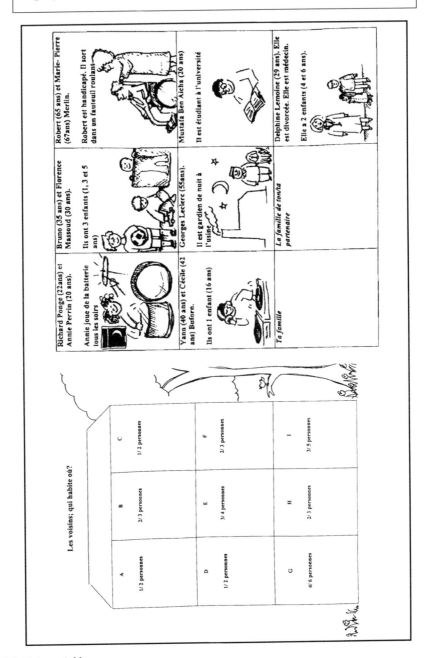

Figure 3.6. Noisy neighbours

This is our list of the simplest form of both topic and interaction language that pupils would need to perform the task. We have added more complicated expressions in brackets.

Topic language

Il/elle a … ans
Mon père/ma mère/il/elle est handicapé(e)/gardien de nuit/étudiant(e)/médecin
Ils ont … enfants/n'ont pas d'enfants
Ils se lèvent/se couchent tôt/tard
Elle joue de la batterie
Il/elle écoute de la musique tous les soirs
Il sort dans un fauteuil roulant

C'est pour 1/2/3 personnes
Il y a 5 personnes dans la/ma famille
C'est trop petit/grand pour 2/3 personnes
Il/elle fait trop de bruit
(Il/elle va déranger … son petit frère/sa petite soeur)
(Il/elle ne va pas déranger …).
Il/elle n'est pas là la nuit

Il doit/ils doivent habiter au rez-de-chaussée
(Pour pouvoir sortir facilement/jouer dans le jardin)
Il peut/ils peuvent habiter au premier étage
Il peut/ils peuvent habiter à côté de …
Il ne peut pas/ils ne peuvent pas habiter à côté de …

Interaction language

On met Bruno et Florence Massoud où?
(Où peut-on placer Bruno et Florence Massoud?)
(Qui peut habiter dans l'appartement A?)
(Moi, je mettrai …) en bas/en haut parce que
Comme ça
D'accord
(Ce sera) C'est difficile/impossible
Ça dépend (de qui on met en haut/bas)
C'est pareil
Essaie …
Mets …
(Ça ne marche pas parce que)
(Il vaut mieux mettre … parce que)
Pourquoi?
Parce que

Similar problem-solving tasks can be devised where, for example, pupils are local estate agents. They have a map of an area and cards with pictures of clients and their housing requirements:

- number of bedrooms
- garden/garage
- town/countryside
- near/far from town centre/beach/mountains, etc.

They have to work together in their group to match people to suitable houses according to their needs and preferences. To offer pupils more opportunity to work independently and to have some say over the task, they can be encouraged to prepare the cards and even the map themselves. They then pass it on to a neighbouring group to do.

4   *Making the problem-solving tasks more complex*

The level of cognitive challenge in the problem-solving tasks discussed so far is relatively low; pupils are dealing with factual information rather than abstract concepts. Even so, for younger pupils to produce the language spontaneously, it is important that the linguistic difficulty of the task is minimised by visual 'props'; the map, the cards with people's requirements and so on. The language is context-embedded; pupils can see what they are doing and if the language fails them, they can simply place the card where they believe it should go. This was also the principle behind the diamond ranking activity for school subjects described in chapter 2 and we will see a further example in chapter 4.

If we want to move pupils on to:

- slightly more open-ended tasks where it is not simply a question of matching people to places on the basis of factual information but also of beginning to express an opinion;
- a point where the 'props', the scaffolding, can be withdrawn;

then we need to do so gradually and to continue to ensure that the linguistic demands are not too difficult. The task in Figure 3.7. is for pupils in groups to agree on arrangements for a party. The language is drawn from very familiar topics and some support is provided through the written prompts. The level of challenge is also reduced because although pupils have to express a personal opinion, it is on fairly basic preferences about food, drink and transport. Again, care would have to be given to identifying and drip-feeding into previous lessons the interaction language required to complete the task.

Topic language

les boissons – du CocaCola? de la bière? du cidre? de l'Orangina?

la nourriture – des sandwichs? du fromage? des baguettes? des pop-corns? des hamburgers? des hotdogs? qui va tout préparer? chacun apporte quelque chose à manger?

le lieu – chez quelqu'un? dans un club de jeunes? en plein air?

le budget – on paie sa part? on paie une entrée?

les invitations – qui est-ce qu'on va inviter? combien d'invités?

les vêtements – en vêtements relax? un bal travesti?

la musique – quelle sorte de musique? une discothèque? un orchestre?

une question de transport – on prend des taxis? on demande aux parents? on y va à pied? à vélo? en autobus?

l'organisation – une personne en est responsable? un groupe de volontaires s'en occupe? chacun s'occupe d'une chose précise?

Figure 3.7. Arranging a party

Moving on one stage further, the task can become more challenging by:

- further reducing the visual support so that the language is *context-reduced*;
- making decisions to be reached more complex and more dependent on opinions about *abstract* concepts;
- requiring the use of language from across a wider range of topic areas.

For example, pupils can just be given a map of a town showing the industrial area, river, park, etc. and they have to agree on where a new school should be built. The more constraints that are added, the more cognitively challenging it becomes, generating discussion and justification of opinions. The industrial area is near the council estate, for example, so if the school were there, pupils would not have so far to walk but the environment would be less pleasant.

Matching the level of difficulty of the task to pupils' ability is clearly no easy matter.

In chapter 4, we will describe some projects carried out by experienced and student teachers with younger pupils. In the case studies, we shall see some examples of basic problem-solving tasks as well as how the teachers identified the interaction language necessary to perform them and built it into the preceding lessons. We shall also examine the outcomes – both the successes and the problems encountered:

- how did pupils respond? Did the tasks succeed in giving them that 'wish to communicate'?

- were the tasks too easy or too difficult for them?
- what was the nature of their language performance? Did they start down the road of developing their strategic competence? Was there a balance to be struck between accuracy and fluency, as Peter Skehan and Pauline Foster suggest in extract 3 of chapter 1?
- And what about the teachers? What difficulties did they meet in trying to implement the ideas discussed here?

We turn now to guided production in action.

> - This chapter has suggested three ways of developing more meaningful tasks. Are some more suitable for beginning teachers to try and others for more experienced teachers?

Note

1   Adapted from *Unité 8, Nouveaux amis: Feuille de travail 9d* (p71) of *Charis Français, Unités 6–10* © The Stapleford Centre, 1997 used with permission. Available from The Stapleford Centre, The Old Lace Mill, Frederick Road, STapleford, Nottingham, NG9 8FN.

Useful follow-up reading

Willis, J. (1996) *A framework for task-based learning.* Harlow: Longman. Gives detailed illustrations of six types of task:

- Listing
- Ordering and sorting
- Comparing
- Problem-solving
- Sharing personal experiences
- Creative tasks.

Rooks, G. (1983) *Conversations sans fin.* Massachusetts: Newbury House. Contains 25 problem-solving tasks, including deciding who should have a heart transplant, which objects best represent life in the USA/France, etc.

The Internet has a wealth of resources on the Francophone countries of Africa. Many charity organisations like Oxfam and Actionaid produce teaching materials in French.

4

Guided language production in action

The second chapter explored ways of presenting and practising language that are more likely to encourage purposeful language use than traditional questioning techniques. Chapter 3 moved us on. Pupils may have been presented with the topic language and may have practised a range of structures. But for what purpose? We suggested that by regularly offering pupils towards the end of a unit of work an opportunity to engage in an extended, genuinely communicative task, we can encourage them to produce all the language that they have learned so far spontaneously. Pupils may be more likely to make the effort to memorise the language during the presentation and practice phases if they know they will be faced by the end of a unit with a chance to use it for themselves. We offered three ways in which guided and carefully structured pair and group oral work can be made more meaningful than the types of activities commonly found in textbooks. Tasks can be made more personally significant, or they can invite pupils to learn something new about the world or they can present them with a problem to be solved using the language. Finally we saw that in order to be able to perform such tasks, pupils not only need the topic language, they also need what we called the *interaction* language. In chapter 2, this tended mainly to be basic commands and requests to each other or the teacher. In chapter 3, it included words and simple phrases for such functions as:

- negotiating with each other (it's your turn/try putting this here);
- giving their opinions (I don't agree with you/it's impossible);
- asking questions (that's important for you; why?);
- giving an appropriate emotional response (that's sad).

We suggested that this language would need to be gradually drip-fed into earlier lessons, if pupils were to be able to use it spontaneously when they performed the task.

But what happens when these ideas are put into practice? What are the issues it raises, both for pupils and for their teachers?

Unfortunately, the timescale of our project meant that we were not able to explore in the classroom all three types of task, since the student teachers we were working with were only in school for six weeks. Furthermore as most of the classes they were assigned to were Key Stage 3, the tasks had to be at a very basic level. We decided to focus on simple problem-solving activities. These will be described in this chapter using a number of case studies. We start by discussing what happened when a student teacher, Elsa Omenetto, her mentor in school, Jane Darcy, and her college tutor set out to explore how to integrate such activities into the scheme of work. The project is discussed by Jane in some detail since what was learned from it formed the framework for the other projects undertaken subsequently by student teachers working in different schools with different age groups and different topic areas. These case studies are described in less depth but are drawn on as the basis for some further suggestions. Finally, since none of us is perfect and there is always something to be learned, we look at some of the problems that can arise; first when working with a group of pupils with Special Educational Needs and then when another class of pupils was faced with a task that was too challenging both linguistically and cognitively.

Case Study 1: Who were the pupils and what were our aims?

The school is a typical large mixed comprehensive school on the outskirts of London with a wide range of intake in terms of pupils' ability. French is taken by all pupils in Year 7, in mixed ability classes until the January of the first year when pupils are divided into sets according to aptitude shown in the first term. The particular class we chose for the project was a top set Year 8 class, as it faced us with a number of challenges:

1   The class had reached the stage where, possibly because they knew each other's ability and there was therefore a certain degree of rivalry and competition, they did not really 'jell' together and the lower-attaining pupils had begun to 'switch off';

2   The textbook on which the scheme of work is based, *Avantage 2*, progresses to the introduction of tenses and more complex sentence structures. It is at this stage where pupils, in our experience, become less confident in pair work, particularly in a top set where pupils want to achieve the same degree of accuracy they managed when dealing with less strenuous single items of vocabulary and the simple, routine exercises of the first book of the course. This lack of confidence can make them unwilling to take risks with the topic language, let alone experiment with spontaneous interaction language.

3   A concern we, like many teachers, had was the restricted amount of time available within the two hours a week modern languages timetable allocation, typical in many schools. How could we develop spontaneous use of the target language as well as:

   • ensure coverage of the other three skills;
   • incorporate grammar teaching;
   • teach dictionary skills, etc?

In the course of the project, we experimented more and more and began to realise that both grammar teaching and the teaching of dictionary skills offer excellent opportunities for promoting spontaneous interaction language. At the outset of the project, however, we were not yet aware of their potential and were concerned that these vital areas might be neglected.

What we were already aware of, however, was that with 32 pupils in the class, a lot of valuable time can be wasted on individual drilling of the basic structure which then rarely stretches beyond very simple and inauthentic pair work activities that are usually *purely formal, devoid of any intention to achieve a result* (Hawkins 1987, p256). There is a fundamental difference between this rather passive language manipulation, where pupils use the **topic language** without any real attempt to adapt it for their own purposes, and more active language production; the *spontaneous speech act with no thought of whether the form is correct or not but simply aimed at solving a problem* (Hawkins 1987, p256). This is the difference between topic language practice and tasks where pupils actually use the language independently in order to convey more personal messages for their own purposes. How is it realistically possible to incorporate such activities into the overcrowded modern languages curriculum? This question was the focus of our project and it is possible!

What were the principles behind our planning?

The keyword in terms of methodology is drip-feeding. Pupils need to be gradually introduced to the interaction language in the presentation and practice phases, so that they can use it later in the production phase spontaneously and automatically. Spontaneity cannot be drilled, but it can be engineered! By working backwards, we would start by identifying the language needed for the final problem-solving task and then introduce it gradually into preceding lessons. The main focus of the initial lessons would, of course, be the **topic language** but pupils would also hear the teacher gradually model more and more phrases that would be useful for the final task. The flow chart in Table 4.1. shows our basic methodology. In the presentation and practice phases, as we have seen in chapter 2, teacher-led activities (TP) lead on to activities in which pupils are supported by the teacher when responding (PT). Activities are then devised in which pupils are given the opportunity to work independently of the teacher (PP), having internalised what the meaning and value of each element is. What is new in this chapter is that in the final guided production stage, when faced with a problem-solving task, they are able to transfer **all** the language to a different context.

Teacher drip-feeds element A of interaction language (TP).

↓

Pupils hear element A and use element A when responding to teacher (PT).

↓

Pupils use element A with each other (PP).

↓

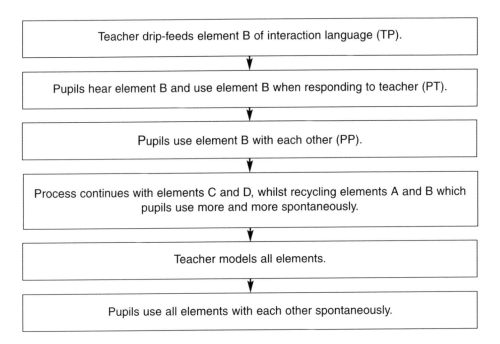

Table 4.1. Flow chart for drip-feeding interaction language

Although each pupil will have internalised the interaction language in different ways and will have deemed certain elements more useful to their individual needs than others, it still means that a genuine target language based classroom is accessible at all levels and by everybody (not just the teacher!) – the ideal which we so rarely achieve. How then does the teacher choose which phrases should be drip-fed? How exactly are they drip-fed? How are they practised?

How did we integrate the principles into the scheme of work?

These are the steps we found to be involved in integrating a problem-solving task into the scheme of work:

1   Decide on which topic language is essential in order both to maintain the continuity of the scheme of work and to carry out a final problem solving task;

2   Decide on a suitable problem-solving task which is centred around the topic language but necessitates pupils using spontaneous interaction language (SIL) amongst themselves in order to carry it out. This should be a communicative activity which promotes purposeful language use;

3   Do the end task ourselves in order to find out what types of SIL phrases would be useful and then simplify the SIL to make it manageable for the pupils;

4   Plan the main topic-based activities whilst also ensuring that they provide opportunities to practise interaction language;

5   Decide on any further topic-based activities that might be needed either to support other skills, or for the end-of-unit test or for evaluating the project as a whole.

We will illustrate these steps now with reference to the textbook and the actual language we decided upon.

1   Choice of topic language

The topic language needed to be taught in depth was centred around personal identification in terms of personality (adjectives and adjectival endings) progressing through to plans for the future (*aller* + infinitive). We realised though that in focussing on these grammar points in particular, other grammar points in the unit would have to be covered more superficially. We hoped that this would be worthwhile in terms of the long-term payoffs; that pupils would have time to really assimilate these grammar points and make them their own, using them spontaneously to express their own meanings.

We felt it was justified to spend time on personality adjectives, since they are important not only as topic language but also for interaction purposes, as they have a strong affective content and so can be used in a number of ways:

- for classroom banter at the start of the lesson; for example, *Gary, tu as l'air anxieux aujourd'hui*. With pupils already familiar with the use of *absent/absente* during the register, this can be extended with Gary referred to as *anxieuse* in order to provoke a reaction! Chapter 5 has some further examples;
- to describe their friends, enemies, pop stars, etc.;
- to enliven a boring role play (at the petrol station, for example) by having a lazy or dynamic pump attendant or a bad-tempered customer.

2   Choice of end activity

As this was our first attempt with problem-solving tasks, we decided that we needed a task that was not too challenging either cognitively or linguistically. We wanted:

- to use as much familiar language as possible;
- plenty of 'props' so that the language would be context-embedded;
- an activity that was fairly practical and straightforward.

So we agreed that pupils should create and use the familiar childhood chatterbox game entitled *Ciel et Enfer* on page 81 of *Avantage 2*. The idea was that these 'chatterboxes' would be used by pupils like crystal balls and would incorporate predictions using near future phrases (*Tu vas* + infinitive).

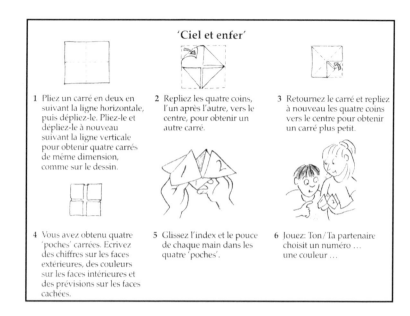

Figure 4.1. Illustration from Avantage 2 (p81) (Heinemann, 1993)

Different groups would prepare different chatterboxes so that every time span in a person's life would be covered. One group would focus on predictions appropriate for the following year, another group for five years' time, another for twenty years and so on. Each member of the group would make their own chatterbox but we insisted that the chatterboxes within each group should be identical. We realised that this constraint was somewhat artificial but we felt it was justifiable in order to promote discussion within the group. The activity would involve pupils making decisions as a group on various aspects of its preparation; which colours and numbers to use on the outside and which phrases were appropriate to use on the inside, according to the time span allotted to their group. The resulting disagreements would hopefully generate plenty of meaningful exchanges!

Having prepared their chatterboxes, pupils would then circulate individually around the class visiting pupils from the different groups in order to gather predictions about their own future in five, ten and twenty years' time. This had the added bonus that pupils would speak to other members of the class in French instead of just their usual pair work partner, and so might improve the class dynamics.

3   Language required for the end activity

We prepared a chatterbox ourselves and used it, noting down the language of our discussion. Our initial list was too hard and had to be simplified to match the level of the class. We have already seen in chapter 3 that teachers tend to anticipate that pupils will need more language than they actually do! Limiting the language should mean that pupils are more likely to become confident and comfortable with what they are offered and therefore more likely to transfer it to new situations and to use it spontaneously.

This was what we agreed was the 'bare bones' necessary to perform the task. It also took into account other language they had learned recently like *c'est vrai/c'est faux/masculin/féminin,* etc.

Deciding on the number and colour	**Quelle couleur/quel numéro?**
Choosing the predictions from a list of possible expressions	**On met ... /On enlève ... /On garde ... , etc.**
Agreeing and disagreeing	**D'accord/Pas d'accord/Pas du tout, etc.**
Explaining the reason for the choice of prediction	**C'est positif/C'est négatif, etc.**

In the event, we realised later that they also needed expressions like:

> **Qu'est-ce qu'on met:**
>
> • **sur les 4 carreaux**
> • **dedans sur les 8 triangles**
> • **comme prédictions?**

This business of identifying the language in advance was more complicated than we had appreciated! On reflection afterwards we thought that perhaps what we should have done is to involve pupils in the process. We could explain to them what the final problem-solving activity would be and spend five minutes brainstorming with them the language they thought they would need. Offering them some say in the language to be learned would help them see the purpose of practising the words they would need and enable them to take greater responsibility for their own learning.

4   Interaction language integrated into topic-based activities

There was a danger that if we embarked on activities, for the sole purpose of practising SIL, they would be perceived by pupils as coming out of the blue. It would also create mental overload, with pupils having to cope with all the new topic language as well as the interaction language. So we had to integrate activities for introducing the SIL into the usual topic-based tasks. This is illustrated in detail in Table 4.2. at the end of this section.

5   Further activities for other skills/assessment

In order to support their writing, pupils would write a description of their friend. We then realised that by modifying this written task slightly, we could create a further opportunity to generate spontaneous language use, which we could assess. So the description would have to include three lies about their friend's personality and their likes and dislikes. They would be encouraged to use their dictionaries to look up any additional adjectives and other expressions they wanted, over and above those that had already been taught. We would present the description to the friend who would have to react by saying what statements they wanted removed. Because there were three of us (student teacher, mentor and college tutor), we could discuss with each pupil their friend's description of them within one lesson. Not only was there therefore a purpose and a context for the writing, pupils' reactions would allow us to assess their speaking skills as one way of measuring the impact of the project as a whole. Figure 4.2. shows a high-attaining pupil's descriptions of her friend, Amber, and the corrections Amber made to the three lies.

Une déscription de Amber

Ma copine s'appelle Amber. A mon avis elle est trés bavarde, assez ouverte et plutôt vive. Je pense qu'elle est aussi asse indépendante, ~~nerveuse~~ timide et plutôt ~~pessimiste~~ optimiste. Elle aime jouer au hockey et faire des courses. Elle n'aime pas les ~~maths~~ sciences et jouer au foot. Elle trés peur des araignée et des scorpion. Elle aimer des chiens, des serpent et des lézard. Elle y a cheveux longs, marron et bouclée. Elle y a les yeux marron. Elle est 13 ans. Elle habite en ville pres de Bromley, en Angleterre.

by Tammy Wright 8PR

Figure 4.2. Tammy's description

Having designed suitable activities, we finally mapped them onto each lesson, inevitably making some last-minute adjustments because of time constraints. Table 4.2 shows the plan for the series of seven lessons carried out in the project school. From left to right:

- column 1 indicates which lesson it was in the series of seven;
- column 2 summarises the topic language which was the main focus of each lesson;
- column 3 shows teacher-led activities, where for example the teacher is asking the class questions;
- column 4 shows activities in which the pupil is using the new language but is **supported** by the teacher;
- column 5 shows activities during which pupils work together independently of the teacher;
- column 6 lists the interaction language practised and then used spontaneously towards the end of the sequence.

T = teacher, Ps =pupils

Topic language	TP	PT	PP	Interaction language
1 Negotiating a weekend outing	Elsa and Jane act out dialogues in order to demonstrate power of intonation and how to agree and disagree.			*D'accord.* *Pas d'accord.*
Personality adjectives: *je suis/tu es.* p76 *Les Signes du Zodiaque*	T demonstrates how to find own sign and how to agree or disagree with characteristics described. e.g. *Je suis Poissons. Oui, d'accord. Je suis farfelue*	Ps feed back their opinions about how their own sign is described by answering teacher. e.g. T: *Tu es Vierge?... Alors, tu es organisé?* P: *Non, pas d'accord.*		*Oui, d'accord.* *Non, pas d'accord.*
Personality adjectives: *il/elle est*	T shows pictures of celebrities: *Alors, David Ginola. Il est paresseux?*	P responds with opinion: *Pas d'accord* and is encouraged to expand to include use of adjective: *Il est sportif.*		
Opinions	T demonstrates how the different adjectives may be placed into *positif* and *négatif* columns following discussion: *Impatient, c'est positif ou négatif?*	P feeds back whether adjectives are positive or negative: *C'est négatif.*	Ps discuss in pairs in which column they should place adjectives: *Amusant. C'est négatif? Non, pas d'accord. C'est positif.*	*C'est positif/ négatif.*
Adjectival agreement: *Il est doux. Elle est douce.*	OHT with *positif* and *négatif* columns and rows *il est ...* and *elle est... .* T demonstrates where to place adjectives whilst explaining grammar rule in target language: *Impatient. C'est positif ou négatif?* (fills in on OHT) *Oui, d'accord, c'est négatif ... alors ...*	Ps contribute by feeding back the positive/negative categorisation they did in pairs earlier: *C'est négatif.*		

	il est impatient. Mais, écoutez et regardez … elle est impatiente. On met un 'e' parce que c'est féminin et on prononce le t.			
	After a few more examples, T expands grammar rule explanation: *'C'est masculin, donc on enlève le e. Mais avec 'pessimiste' et 'artistique', on garde le e, même si c'est masculin.'*	Ps respond to incorrect adjectives by T: *Pas d'accord C'est masculin. On enlève le e.*		*C'est masculin. C'est féminin.* *On met … On enlève … On garde …*
2 Adjectival agreement consolidation	T explains and demonstrates *Cherche l'intrus.* **(The game is explained in full following this table)**	Ps play game, explaining their choices.	Ps create own version of *Cherche l'intrus.*	Spontaneous use of all above SIL
Likes and dislikes p79. *J'aime … Je n'aime pas … J'ai peur de …* and transfer to *il/elle.*	Having completed a listening exercise involving *je* structures, T uses questions to elicit the transfer to *il/elle: il aime regarder la télé. D'accord?*	Ps feed back answers to listening exercise using *il/elle: Pas d'accord. Il aime écouter de la musique.*		*D'accord. Pas d'accord.*
	T sets a written homework where pupils are asked to write a description of their partner incorporating personality adjectives and likes and dislikes but which has three lies in it.			
3	T shows written descriptions of celebrities containing errors and encourages ps to correct mistakes in target language.	Ps correct errors by telling teacher the mistakes: *David Beckham. C'est masculin. On enlève ve et on met f – sportif.*		

		Ps then self-correct their written homework.		*On met …* *On enlève …*
Near future: *Je vais …* + infinitive. (weekend activities)	T presents flashcards to introduce vocabulary of weekend activities.			
	T encourages pupils to match ends of sentences with infinitives on OHT.	Ps tell teacher which ends of sentences go with which infinitives. *On met* rendre visite *avec* à ma soeur.		*On met … avec* *On enlève …*
4 Near future: *Tu vas …* + infinitive (prediction type activities) p77		Ps complete matching exercise (ex.4) which links speech bubbles (*je vais …*) with (*tu vas …*) and feed back to T.		
		Ps complete French/English paradigm of *aller=* to go, matching verb to subject pronoun.		*On met …* *avec …*
C'est pour dans un/cinq/ dix an(s)	T discusses future life events with pupils: *Tu vas avoir un enfant … C'est pour … dans un an?*	Ps react and respond when these life events take place in their opinion: *Pas d'accord. C'est pour dans dix ans.*	Ps ask each other when these life events take place and fill in a grid.	*C'est pour … dans … an(s).* *D'accord. Pas d'accord.*
5	T acts out agreeing on format of chatterbox game, and then shows a summary of the language needed on OHT.		Ps create chatterbox game, agreeing on format. **(A transcript of a game-making conversation is provided in the Results section)**	Spontaneous use of all SIL
6	T acts out how to play the chatterbox game.		Ps go round and find their horoscopes for	Spontaneous use of all SIL

			1/5/10/20 years time by playing the chatterbox game.	
			(A transcript of a game-playing conversation is provided in the Results section)	Spontaneous use of all SIL.
7		Ps feed back the horoscopes they collected last lesson using *je vais* ... Ps then write up their horoscopes.		
	T shows descriptions written by their partner in lesson 2 and gets them to react and change them as a test of their spontaneous use of SIL.			Spontaneous use of SIL *on enlève/on garde/on met* ...
		Ps complete questionnaire on what they thought of the project.		

Table 4.2. Plan for seven lessons

An example of one activity in practice: *cherche l'intrus*

Yes, the practice is always more useful to teachers than the theory, so here goes!

This is an excellent activity to illustrate the drip-feeding methodology as it progresses **within itself** from being a teacher-led activity (TP) through to pupil-teacher (PT) feedback and eventually to pupils devising similar examples for themselves in pairs (PP).

The aim of this activity is:

a   to revise *d'accord* and *pas d'accord*
b   to encourage pupils to use *on met/on enlève* since these are key expressions needed for the final problem-solving task.

a Background

It should be clear from Table 4.2. that pupils had already **heard** SIL *on met/on enlève/on garde* and *masculin/féminin* before the game, since the grammar point of adjectival agreements had been explained by the teacher in the target language, for example:

On met un 'e' parce que c'est féminin et on prononce le 't'.
On enlève le 'e' parce que c'est masculin.
On garde le 'e' même si c'est masculin.

However, they had not yet used it themselves. The use of the target language by the teacher for explaining one particular grammar point can therefore provide a context for exposing pupils to another, as we shall see again in chapter 5.

Personality adjectives had been introduced in an earlier lesson in which pupils were encouraged to voice their opinions (using *d'accord/pas d'accord*) on famous people's personalities.

b Creating and playing *cherche l'intrus* with the teacher

In this activity, three lists of various personality adjectives are displayed horizontally on an OHT followed by a box for the odd one out (*'l'intrus'*). The teacher models *on enlève/on met* with mime when discussing with the pupils which words should be **taken from** the list and **put into** the odd one out box. The title of the game will need to be explained, of course. A particular adjective could be deemed as the odd one out for a variety of reasons (positive/negative, masculine/feminine, etc). It is best to stick to one reason for the first three rows of adjectives.

						L'INTRUS
1	impatient	coléreux	pessimiste	nerveux	amusant	
2	sportif	obstiné	organisé	indépendant	sympa	
3	actif	travailleur	farfelu	original	optimiste	
4						
5						

Oui, d'accord/non, pas d'accord responses (previously learnt) are elicited from pupils by proposing one of the words as appropriate for the odd one out box. Then the reasons why are examined. The question *Pourquoi?* should elicit a *c'est …* response although pupils will probably need prompting. They may well need the whole process demonstrated to them both verbally and visually for row one in order to understand the concept, as this example from our lesson shows:

Teacher–Pupil (TP)
input of SIL

T: *Numéro 1. Quel est l'intrus? Qu'est-ce qu'on met dans la case l'intrus? On met impatient? Amusant?*

P: (either silence or a guess or correct answer)

T: *Amusant? D'accord? Oui?...* (awaits class response) *Oui, d'accord! On enlève* (mimes) *amusant et on met amusant dans la case l'intrus.*

Pourquoi? Pourquoi amusant?

P: (silence!)

T: *Amusant, c'est positif ou négatif? C'est ...*

P: *Positif!*

T: *Oui, c'est positif. Et pessimiste, c'est ...?*

P: *Négatif!*

T: *Oui, d'accord. Pessimiste, c'est négatif. Et impatient?*

P: *C'est négatif.*

T: *Oui, exactement.* (goes through whole list) *Alors on enlève amusant parce que c'est positif et les autres sont négatifs. D'accord? ... et on met amusant dans la case l'intrus. Très bien.*

Teacher now uses mime to prompt pupils to produce *on enlève/on met* themselves with a choral response:

T: *Numéro 2. Quel est l'intrus? Qu'est-ce qu'on met dans la case l'intrus?*

On met sportif dans la case l'intrus? D'accord ou pas d'accord?

Pupil–Teacher
(PT) use
of SIL

P: *Pas d'accord. Obstiné!*

T: *Pourquoi?*

P: *C'est négatif!*

T: *Et sportif?*

P: *C'est positif!*

T: *Et sympa?*

P: *C'est positif!*

T: *Tu peux m'expliquer en français? On ...*(mimes) *...*

P: *enlève*

T: *Oui, on enlève ...*(points to chosen word)

P: *obstiné*

T: *Oui, on enlève obstiné et on ...* (mimes)

P: *met*

T: *Oui, on met obstiné ... dans la case l'intrus* (mimes).

Donne-moi la phrase complète, s'il te plaît.

> P: (with teacher prompting by mime and pointing) ***On enlève*** *obstiné et **on met** obstiné dans la case l'intrus.*
> T: *Excellent!! Pourquoi?*
> P: *C'est négatif.*
> T: *D'accord et les autres sont ...*
> P: *Positifs.*

Further practice then continues with row number three but with a bit less support from the teacher.

c Playing *cherche l'intrus* **with each other (positive/negative)**

Pupils then devise further questions themselves (rows four and five), using SIL with support from the teacher (TP to PT) if needed, all the while incorporating the SIL *d'accord/pas d'accord/on met/on enlève.*

d Playing *cherche l'intrus* **with each other (masculine/feminine)**

Rows six and seven are then displayed which contain adjectives for which the positive/negative response is not appropriate, as the lists contain words which are the odd one out because they are masculine or feminine instead. This therefore becomes an exercise in which a grammar point is reinforced alongside SIL, the topic language of personality adjectives being the main focus:

e.g.

						L'INTRUS
6	généreuse	dynamique	rieur	ouverte	douce	
7	optimiste	anxieux	fonceur	impulsive	réservé	

Giving pupils greater choice

Pupils work in pairs to produce activities where the words and the reason for the odd one out are chosen by themselves using SIL (PP). They are then asked to swap books and actually complete the exercise created by another pair. This gives them some freedom in choosing what to write and an audience and a purpose for it. It also allows the teacher to circulate and assess their progress, by asking them to explain why they have put a particular choice in the odd one out box. Pupils are therefore gaining experience of using SIL at all levels (TP, PT and PP). This is preparing them all the time for the problem-solving task which is exclusively PP in groups instead of pairs and in which pupils should hopefully be able to produce the language, without having to think about it, as they have been exposed to it sufficiently in meaningful contexts.

Results of the project: what did the pupils make of it?

In planning our project, we were concerned to gather as much evidence as we could of its impact on pupils' learning and particularly on the development of their speaking skills. Clearly we could not undertake rigorous, systematic research but we wanted to try to ensure that our own enthusiasm for the project did not colour too much our judgements! Apart from the task where pupils had to change statements in the description their friend had written, we also used:

- video of lessons, extracts of which we transcribed;
- field notes that we made directly after the lesson, jotting down our albeit subjective impressions;
- a questionnaire. This included closed questions such as whether pupils thought they had spoken more/less/the same French during the project than in the previous lessons, and also more open-ended questions such as what they liked and disliked about the project;
- a brief interview with six pupils, allowing us to probe in more depth similar questions to those on the questionnaire. We also asked them what advice they would give to other pupils about speaking French.

Here we summarise some of the points that seemed most significant to us.

Video extracts

Pupils were video'ed both when they were making the chatterbox game and when they were playing it. In this first extract, Robbie, Chris and Tom are making chatterboxes. They are trying to make sure that each of them has the same colours, with the same predictions underneath them. Chris has just discovered that Tom has a different colour from him and Robbie. Interaction language is printed in bold, language learned from previous topics or in other contexts is underlined. To take just one example, they had learned *changer* in the context of a prediction that they would *changer de look* in ten years' time but Chris uses it here to insist that Tom changes the colour on his chatterbox.

Chris: (pointing at Tom's chatterbox) *Changer le rose, changer le rose ...*

Robbie: *Tu vas gagner ... Changer le couleur?* (sees Tom's) ... *Lève* (meaning *enlève*) *le ...*

Chris: **Lève** *le noir.*

Robbie: **Mets** *le ... mets le ... le rose.*

*Violet, c'est ... tu vas ... tu vas avoir beaucoup de chance, **d'accord ou pas d'accord?** Tu vas avoir beaucoup de chance, **d'accord ou pas d'accord?***

Robbie: *Tu vas acheter, tu vas acheter une belle maison.*

Chris: *Changer, changer, changer.*

Robbie: *Tu vas acheter un nouveau infant* (you'll buy a new kid – laughs). *Tu vas, tu vas avoir tres enfants, **d'accord ou pas d'accord?***

Chris: **Pas d'accord,** *changer.*

Robbie: **Pas d'accord? Pourquoi, pourquoi pas d'accord?**

Tom:	*Aller <u>Etats Unis, Etats Unis</u>.*
Chris:	**Parce que, parce que ...**
Tom:	*<u>Excusez moi, Etats Unis, Etats Unis</u>.*
Robbie:	*Non, non, tu vas avoir tres enfants.*
Tom:	*En prison, en prison.*
Chris:	*C'est non **négatif** ... oui, oui, prison, prison.*
Robbie:	*C'est **positif**.Qu'est-ce que ... couleur?*

- Compare this extract of the pupils talking to Willis' comment about the importance of meaning-focussed activities in extract 7 of chapter 1. To what extent do you feel these pupils are performing the task *on automatic pilot without really having to think about what they mean?*

- Are the pupils using any of the communication strategies listed in extract 8 of chapter 1?

It is very hard to capture on paper the pupils' enthusiasm, genuine wish to communicate and even their ability to make jokes in the target language. This extract was in fact part of a conversation within the group that lasted approximately four minutes, all in French. It is noticeable that these pupils were less reliant on stock phrases and incorporated the underlined vocabulary they had previously learned in several other different contexts into the one conversation, as well as the interaction language actually taught. The same is true of the class as a whole, though not all the groups managed to sustain conversations of this length. The results differed not just according to attainment level but also personality; extrovert, risk-taking pupils being more willing to 'have a go' than shyer pupils or those who preferred to 'play it safe', feeling that they had to be accurate. At no point, though, was the use of this wider range of vocabulary discussed, revised or rehearsed. Its use is completely spontaneous and seemed to provide evidence that pupils can activate vocabulary from a wide range of topic areas if on some level they have deemed it relevant, and they are faced with a task that calls it into play. It appeared that our decision to choose a relatively easy problem-solving task, both linguistically and cognitively, was justified.

In the next extract, Robbie decides to chat about buying new trainers in the middle of the teacher's explanation ... but it *is* in French!

Robbie:	*<u>J'ai besoin de </u>nouveaux baskets pour lundi.*
	(Chris looks puzzled.) *Des baskets.*
Chris:	*<u>Je ne comprends pas</u>.* (Robbie points to his shoes.)
Robbie:	*Lundi. <u>C'est mega-cool</u>.*

Here, Bonnie, Claire, Louise and Sabrina are busy preparing their chatterboxes. They are deciding which prediction to put on which part of the paper:

Bonnie:	*Changer de look?*

Claire:	*Oui.*
Bonnie:	*<u>A</u> tu vas <u>un accent</u>?*
Claire:	*Oui.*
Bonnie:	*This way … err … <u>à droite</u>?*
Claire:	*Oui!*
Louise:	*<u>Numéro six…numéro six?</u>*
Bonnie:	*<u>Numéro six…</u> tu vas changer de look.*
Sabrina:	*Non!*
Bonnie:	*Oui. Tu vas changer de look.*
Louise:	*Oui!*
Sabrina:	*Non!*
Claire:	*Oui, je **garde**.*

- Is there any evidence in these conversations that pupils are beginning to *unpack* the unanalysed chunks that Rosamond Mitchell refers to in extract 2 of chapter 1?

And finally, Robbie is finding out about his horoscope from Pascal:

Robbie:	*<u>Numéro dix.</u>*
Pascal:	*<u>Un, deux, trois, quatre, cinq, six, sept, huit, neuf, dix.</u>*
Robbie:	*<u>Le vert</u>.*
Pascal:	***D'accord*** *… Tu vas gagner au loto!*
Teacher:	*Alors?*
Robbie:	*C'est <u>super</u>!*
Pascal:	*<u>Acheter un dictionnaire</u>!!*
Robbie:	*Ah non!*

There are certainly plenty of errors in these extracts! Look back to chapter 1 and in particular to Peter Skehan and Pauline Foster's research in extract 3.

- What do you think are the causes of these errors in terms of the balance between fluency, accuracy and complexity?
- How would you address them? Would you correct them at the time or make an internal note of the most common and take them up later?

Field notes

We were in the privileged position of there being three of us in the classroom for most lessons: myself, Elsa and her college tutor. I think that having a student teacher can really offer something to the mentor. It gives him or her the opportunity to try something new but with extra support if it all goes horribly wrong! It also meant that we could keep field notes, jotting down impressions either during the lesson itself, or straight afterwards. This is what the college tutor wrote:

> *I am very struck as it is a long time since I saw pupils genuinely struggling to communicate, rather than simply 'going through the motions'. It was something about the expressions on their faces; it was like they had made the language 'their own' rather than something the teacher had popped into their mouths. When they were stuck, instead of the usual complaining in English, they were going for it in French. Sabrina's really come on – you can't stop her talking! She came up to me at the end of the lesson and told me her grandmother speaks French Creole and she learned it at primary school. Yet I know from Jane that up to now she has been very unmotivated. What was it about the experiences of the project that allowed her to use all this language, almost like unleashing something?*

- How do these observations relate to Michael Grenfell's point about language as *an expression of sense of self* in extract 4 of chapter 1?

Summary of impressions from questionnaires, interviews, written and spoken tasks and videos

From the questionnaires, the interviews, the videos as well as from the various written and spoken tasks we set them, our experience was that giving pupils access to interaction language and the opportunities to use it in meaningful contexts resulted in a marked improvement both in the motivation and the progress of the class as a whole.

In terms of improvement in **motivation**:

- in the questionnaire, 65% of the pupils said that the project had made them like French more;

- the pace of the lesson was 'hot'. Pupils could not wait to get on with the oral pair and group tasks set. They tried to start the tasks before they had been fully explained on many occasions and it was sometimes difficult to stop them at the end!

- it seemed that pupils stayed on task longer than during typical activities before the project;

- they wanted to experiment with different vocabulary and became more willing to use a dictionary;

- they became much more confident and more willing to take risks as some of these comments on the questionnaire indicate:

> – *Before the project I was very nevers and now I am a bit more confedence.*
> – *I'm not afraid now to make a mistake. It's best to have a go, make a guess and try things out; after all you've got nothing to lose.*

- pupils themselves commented on the new opportunities they felt had been given to them in terms of real communication. Sabrina, for example, said how she had managed to hold a conversation with some French boys she had met in Bromley. One boy wrote on the questionnaire: *It made me speak more like a native Frenchman.*

As to **linguistic progress:**

- in the questionnaire, 81% of pupils said that they had spoken more French during pair work than they usually did before. 50% said that they chatted less in English during pair work now (whether they are to be believed is, of course, another matter!);

- the language seemed to become more real for them, encouraging them to say and write what they really wanted to. For example, Paul extended a homework task of saying what he thought would happen in the future by stating the actual type of ideal partner he would like to meet;

- they seemed to become more aware of grammar and therefore more capable of manipulating the language not just in speaking tasks but also in written tasks, as Tammy's description of Amber suggests;

- an unexpected outcome was that the pupils interviewed said that they felt their listening skills had improved. Presumably this was because in the tasks we had set them they genuinely needed to know what the other group members were saying in order to respond appropriately. Compare this to the traditional role play of shopping for food, for example, where as long as you say your 'part' and ask for a tin of peas, it does not really matter whether you do or do not understand the price.

- as I was so impressed with their progress, I decided at the end of the year that they would take a practice Foundation GCSE in Listening, Speaking and Reading and also undertake the necessary written coursework. The vast majority of the class gained A–C grades.

Other areas of progress

- Their social skills improved. There was a noticeable difference in the group dynamics now that they had all worked with each other and been encouraged to take risks in the language, without fear of being laughed at;

- They were able to work more independently and this surely lies at the heart of spontaneous interaction.

We have described the project in some detail. It may be useful now to look briefly at how similar principles can be applied to different topics. For ease of reference, some of the projects of the student teachers are summarised in the same tabular form as this project. Because they tended to be working with Year 7 to Year 9 pupils, the problem-solving tasks remain fairly basic. However, we hope that they show how elements of both topic language and interaction language can be presented and practised in each lesson. At any stage, of course, further ideas for presenting and practising the language, offered in chapter 2, could also be integrated. When we undertook our projects, we were not aware of them all, particularly those related to developing pupils' awareness of the written form of the language!

Case Study 2

In her first teaching practice placement, Sandra Viegas had noted that:

> *I managed after a couple of weeks to get the pupils used to* me *using the target language but it was hard to get them to speak French amongst themselves. They were not used to doing it and they did not want to look or sound silly when speaking French.*

So when she moved on to her second placement, she decided to undertake a project on encouraging spontaneous use of the target language. She was working with a Year 7, middle set, in a girls' comprehensive school in East London, where most of the pupils came from a range of ethnic backgrounds. The topic was *House and Home*. She decided that the aim of the final problem-solving activity would be:

- to complete a diamond ranking exercise where pupils could choose and then prioritise the ten 'ideal' rooms they would like to have in their home (for example, a swimming pool or an ice cream shop);
- to complete a picture of a house, showing exactly where five of the 'ideal' rooms would be placed.

Because the topic is a sensitive one in an area of London noted for its poor housing, she felt that this was more appropriate than asking pupils to discuss their own homes.

Topic language	TP	PT	PP	Interaction language
1 Revision of towns, countries, *j'habite à ... en ...*				
2 *En ville, à la campagne montagne,* etc	T introduces vocabulary. through flashcards encouraging pupils to ask: *c'est quoi en français 'countryside?'*			

	T shows small section of flashcard. One pupil guesses what it is. T asks class: *d'accord ou pas d'accord?*			*D'accord, pas d'accord.* *Encore un peu.*
3 *Une ferme, un chalet, etc.*	Listening; ps match number of flashcard to word teacher says. T begins to correct the activity: *numéro 1, c'est une ferme, d'accord?*		Ps ask each other: *numéro 2, c'est un chalet, d'accord?*	*Numéro 1,2 etc.* *D'accord, pas d'accord.*
4 *La cuisine, la salle à manger, etc.*	Similar activities. Then T matches picture of room on board to written card: *on met cette carte ici, d'accord?*	Ps volunteer to match remaining cards.		*On met ... ici*
	T plays *cherche l'intrus* (e.g. *la chambre, la cuisine, la salle à manger, le jardin*)	Ps answer: *on met le jardin dans la case intrus.*		*On met ... dans la case.*
5 *En bas, en haut, à gauche/droite*	Pupils have a written description of house. T follows description, placing cards of rooms onto house outline on board and asking: *on met la cuisine en bas, à gauche, d'accord?* He or she sometimes makes a deliberate mistake to provoke *non, pas d'accord, à droite.*	Ps volunteer to place remaining cards.		*On met ... en bas, à gauche; d'accord?*
Homework; to choose five rooms for an 'ideal house', draw them on square cards and find the French words				
6 Revision and teaching ten most popular 'ideal' rooms	T mouths words, pupils lip read. T answers *d'accord* or *pas d'accord.* T then deliberately		P1 mouths words, P2 lip reads. P1 answers *d'accord* or	*D'accord, pas d'accord.* *Moins vite.*

	says word too fast to provoke *moins vite.*		*pas d'accord.*	
7	T models diamond ranking, placing his or her ideal rooms in order of priority. Then he or she asks pupils their opinion *où est-ce qu'on met la piscine?*	Ps answer: *on met ... en numéro 1.* Teacher asks *pourquoi?* to provoke *c'est plus important que la patinoire.*	Ps complete own diamond ranking, placing ideal rooms in order of priority.	*On met ... en numéro 1. C'est plus/ moins important.*
8 All topic language + *à côté de. On met la piscine en bas, à côté du garage*			Ps place five ideal rooms onto plan of house.	Spontaneous use of all SIL

Table 4.3. Plan of lessons for House and Home

The following is an extract from a group of pupils carrying out the diamond ranking activity. Interaction language is indicated in bold. Sandra comments:

> *I was really impressed by their use of French. Some really put effort into doing the activity, trying their best to use French only. Others at least used different intonation and varied their tone of voice to try to get their message over. One could say that the interaction language used was quite limited and basic but one cannot forget that acquiring features of the language is a long process. Over a short period of time, pupils have internalised simple language and made it their own in order to use it spontaneously to interact with each other, negotiate meanings and express basic opinions.*

Une salon ... **moins important ou plus important?***
Moins important.
En bas?
D'accord.
*Shop **moins important ou plus important?***
Moins important, moins important.
Moins important.
Numéro sept, huit, neuf, dix?
Numéro sept; d'accord ou pas d'accord?
D'accord.

* pupil error

It is interesting to note that this next group of pupils transferred the language they had just learned for placing rooms in a house (*en haut, en bas*) to the new context of placing rooms on the diamond, thus providing themselves with a 'short cut' to going through all the numbers.

Une piscine... <u>au milieu ou ... en bas?</u>
En bas.
Numéro sept?
D'accord.
Le magasin de glaces, <u>au milieu ou en bas</u>?
En bas.
<u>*Une salle de jeux, en haut, au milieu ou en bas*</u>*?*
<u>*Au milieu.*</u>
Numéro cinq?
Cinq ... oui.

In the next extract, pupils are deciding where the rooms they have chosen should go:

Le cinéma ... <u>en haut ou en bas?</u>
<u>*En haut.*</u>
*À côté de salle ... salle de bains ... **d'accord ou pas d'accord?***
D'accord ... *la discothèque ... <u>en haut ou en bas?</u>*
<u>*Au milieu.*</u>
*À côté de un salon ... **d'accord ou pas d'accord?***
D'accord.

- Which words and expressions do pupils seem more confident with? Why?
- Which words that have been taught are not used? Why?

Sandra gave the pupils a questionnaire to complete. The results, along with Sandra's comments, are given below. You may want to compare your conclusions about the language they used most to theirs.

Some facts and figures

Question 1: Examples of the vocabulary used most during the activities.

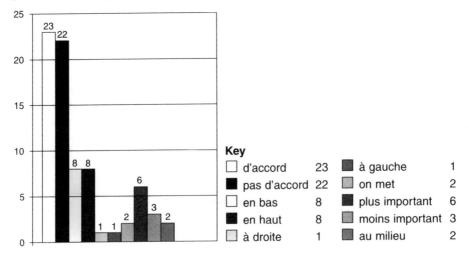

Key

☐ d'accord	23	▨ à gauche	1
■ pas d'accord	22	▨ on met	2
☐ en bas	8	■ plus important	6
■ en haut	8	▨ moins important	3
▨ à droite	1	▨ au milieu	2

Sandra comments:

> *All pupils were able to mention more than two expressions, which was really encouraging. The expressions they mentioned as using most frequently (**d'accord, pas d'accord**) were the ones that were first introduced, so they had many opportunities to be reinforced in the course of the subsequent lessons. Surprisingly the expression **on met** was mentioned three times, more than **à gauche** and **à droite**, although I had the impression that they tended to rely on nouns rather than verbs to get their message over. There is always a danger with questionnaires that pupils may not remember accurately what they did!*

Question 2

The project made them like French more/less/just the same:

- 56% said *the same*;
- 44.4% said *more*;
- no one answered *less.*

Question 3

The activity they enjoyed most was:

- 51.8% preferred placing the rooms in the house;
- 29.6% preferred doing the diamond ranking activity;
- 18.6% enjoyed both activities equally.

It may be that one of the reasons for the popularity of the house activity was that it came at the end of the sequence of lessons, when pupils had become more familiar with the interaction language.

Question 4

92.6% of pupils said that the activities had helped them to express themselves in French. When asked in what way:

- *more confidence* was mentioned 36.6% times;
- *they could understand each other better* was mentioned 33.3% times;
- *they had had opportunities to use the language for a real reason* was mentioned 30% times.

Perhaps they felt the activities had helped them to understand better because they were practical, involving moving rooms around on paper, so that everyone could see what they were referring to. When children learn their first language, we usually talk about 'the here and now'; things that are visible like clothes, toys, food, etc which help them to make sense of the noises we are making!

Question 5

> **When doing pair work, they spoke ... French than usual:**
>
> - 77% said *more French*;
> - 22.3% said *the same amount*;
> - no one answered *less French*.
>
> *Because they had practised the expressions they needed to do the task, pupils probably felt confident enough to use more French than they usually do. Perhaps they also felt they had spoken more French because the activities were quite demanding and they had to have quite long exchanges to negotiate a common agreement.*

Question 6

> **When doing partner work, they chatted ... in English than usual.**
>
> - 67% said they had chatted *less* in English;
> - 22.2% said *the same*;
> - 14.8% said they had chatted *more*.
>
> *The reasons for some pupils using English more may be linked to their answers to the next question, which asked them what they found hardest about speaking French with their partners. Many mentioned pronunciation. They also said that they would have liked to say certain things but they did not know how to say them in French.*

The reported difficulties with pronunciation seem to lend support to the importance of the kinds of activities described in section 4 of chapter 2. Sandra's last comment raises one of the central dilemmas in encouraging spontaneous language use. The very process of becoming genuinely interested in what they are talking about means that pupils may want to move beyond the language that has been so carefully identified, presented and practised. For some, this may mean reverting to English. But we can try to exploit more fully pupils' desire to say what they want to say:

- by inviting them to make suggestions during the presentation phase, *c'est quoi en français ...?*;
- by writing any other words that are asked for during a lesson on a poster;
- by helping them to find their way around a dictionary;
- by encouraging them to use the textbook as a personal learning resource (pupils often do not even know, for example, how to use the Contents list at the front of the book);
- by encouraging them to research and prepare a presentation on a topic of particular interest to them. Larry Vandergrift and Claire Bélanger (1998) have some very useful suggestions as to how to provide pupils with clear guidelines on giving a presentation.

Chapter 5 will suggest other ways in which pupils can be helped to cope, when what they want to say falls outside their linguistic repertoire.

Sandra's observation on question 4 about children learning their first language seems to lend further support to the idea of using visual 'props' to make the task less challenging. This was also a feature of case study 3.

Case Study 3

Like Sandra, **Christine Peuby and Maria Rejiba** worked with a Year 7 class and on the topic of *House and Home* but theirs was a mixed ability class in a mixed comprehensive school in North East London. In devising a final problem-solving activity, they decided that some form of game would be appropriate since:

> low self-esteem and high anxiety reduces motivation, and it is important to create a safe environment where pupils would feel more comfortable and therefore confident to express themselves in the target language. From our previous teaching practice, we knew that games contribute to a relaxed happy atmosphere and are a natural way of communicating, especially for Year 7 pupils. They appeal to their sense of fun and motivation is increased because they want to win or at least have a go.

The aim of their final problem-solving activity was to play a game, based on the TV series *Through the keyhole*. Working in groups of three or pairs, pupils would first choose a famous personality and draw their house, with clues of related family members or favourite objects hidden under paper flaps of windows and doors. The other pair would then have to establish the identity of the personality by asking questions such as: *C'est un homme? Il habite en Angleterre?*. They could ask for *un indice* at which point one of the flaps would be briefly uncovered. If they wanted to see it for longer, they had to say *moins vite* or *encore une fois*. If they managed to guess correctly, they could announce *on a gagné, vous avez perdu*.

Similar activities to those described in Sandra's project were used to present and practise the language. A particular feature of Christine and Maria's project, however, was the initial **Awareness-raising**. They felt that it was worthwhile devoting a lesson to enabling the pupils to understand what they meant by spontaneous use of the language. Pupils were shown a short clip from the BBC video *Vive la différence* (*BBC Learning Zone Teaching MFL*; Part 1). The clip showed an extract from a French and Saunders programme, where the two women, having embarked on learning Italian by listening to cassettes, concluded that they were now sufficiently competent to be able to talk to each other only in Italian. Of course, they find they have to resort to mime and saying English words with an Italian accent. Pupils thoroughly enjoyed the extract and reported finding similar problems when faced with pair work in the classroom.

A second awareness-raising activity was a pelmanism game played in groups, with one of the group acting as a 'police officer', noting down the words or phrases where pupils resorted to English. The resulting list was useful not only to the student teachers in terms of drawing up their list of SIL language. It also helped the pupils to understand that what it means to **really** speak French is not just the set phrases of the topic covered but all the everyday expressions they would normally use with each other.

Christine and Maria noted that not **all** the pupils were able to transfer **all** the interaction language to the final activity. The following extract from the video they made shows the most successful group of pupils playing the game, as they ask for each of the flaps to be revealed.

Hersharon	***A moi.***
Safia	***A toi.***
Sam	*C'est un garçon.*
Safia	*Oui.*
Adam	***Un indice*** *s'il vous plaît.*
Hersharon	***Moins vite.***
Adam	***Encore une fois.***
Sam	***Un indice*** *s'il vous plaît.*
Hersharon	***Encore une fois, moins vite.***
Adam	*Teletubbies?*
Safia	*This one, this one.*
Adam	*C'est Tinky Winky.*
Safia	*Non.*
Sam	***Un indice*** *s'il vous plaît.*
Safia	*It's the last one.*
Sam	*David Beckham.* ***On a gagné. Vous avez perdu.***

The video also showed that a group of lower attainers were slower and less accurate and were constantly looking for the visual support displayed on the classroom walls. However, Christine and Maria note that:

> *if in general the low attainers were less likely than the high attainers to pick up and use* ***all*** *the interaction language in the game, some of them were more willing to spontaneously reproduce single words in the preceding lessons than some of the high attainers, who did not seem to put in as much effort. Perhaps the reason for this lies in the fact that these low attainers had very poor writing skills and were therefore very motivated to communicate orally. The interactive classroom environment gives them the opportunity to express themselves which they enjoy immensely.*

Christine and Maria's final comments below appear to relate to extract 10 of chapter 1, where Grenfell and Harris discuss differences between risk-takers and those who prefer to 'play it safe':

> *It seems that personality and learning styles are a significant factor in determining the use of interaction language. Those pupils who were generally more lively in nature and liked participating in oral topic-based activities anyway were those who had more confidence to spontaneously use the interaction language.*

Consider the pupils in one of your classes.
- Which ones seem the most and least likely to use the language spontaneously?
- Does it relate to their personality and learning styles, as well as their attainment level?
- Have you found that games encourage them to 'take risks' with the language?

Like Sandra, Christine and Maria noted that the language used most often in the final activity was the language they had learned in the first half of the project that had been extensively practised. Words and expressions with a strong affective content, like *tricheur* and *on a gagné* were also popular. The sound of words may also be a factor in retaining them. In the course of the project, they had taught the pupils some of the filler/hesitation devices discussed by Zoltan Dörnyei in extract 9 of chapter 1; words like *bof*, for example. One pupil commented *it is so funny that it sticks in your head.* Fortuitously, the day after the final activity, a football match was arranged with French pupils on an exchange visit. Christine and Maria were delighted when they heard some of their pupils chorus triumphantly *on a gagné* and *vous avez perdu!*

Case Study 4

Emer McKenna worked with a Year 9 class in a North London comprehensive school, with pupils from a range of ethnic backgrounds. The class was a mixed ability group with some high-attaining pupils. Her comments on her experiences during her first teaching practice help to remind us of the link between independent language **use** and independent language **learning** discussed in extract 13 of chapter 1:

> *Why is it that pupils in so many classes do not seem to pass a certain point in achievement? They know quite a lot but they cannot use it to express their own meanings. Real interaction in the classroom, I think, requires the teacher to step out of the limelight, to cede a full role to the pupils in developing and carrying through activities and to be tolerant of the errors pupils make whilst attempting to communicate. Teacher-centred classrooms cannot, by their very nature, be interactive classrooms. A lot of textbooks present the language in interesting ways but for many pupils, the foreign language is what is in the book; it is predictable, can be learned by heart and reproduced in manageable chunks. As modern languages teachers, we know that language is not like that. Very few pupils have the opportunity to make the language a reality. This was the challenge for my second teaching practice.*

The topic was *Town and Countryside.* At the end of the topic, pupils were to research and then give a presentation on their chosen town or region of France. The class was not used to using interaction language so, even though this was a Year 9 class, Emer wanted to keep the task simple both linguistically and cognitively so that they would have a feeling of success from this first opportunity of using the language spontaneously. She decided, therefore, to introduce it through a simple board game, with plenty of visual support and that both the topic language and the language used for the game itself would be relatively basic. In the event, the final case study in this chapter suggests this was a wise decision. The board game showed pictures of various buildings in the town. If, when they landed on them, the pupils could not say a full sentence about the picture, they missed their next turn. In addition, there were 'Chance' cards with a range of instructions or questions. Some of these required pupils to refer to authentic brochures in order to find the answer. The winner was the first person to reach the exit from the town. Emer was pleased that during the game even the low attainers said more than they normally would. As in Christine and Maria's project, those words with a high affective content like *tu triches* and *j'en ai marre* were the most popular expressions. As one pupil said of *j'en ai marre*: *It's nice to know how to say such a normal everyday expression. I like the way it sounds too!* Emer felt that although the interaction language itself was fairly simple, pupils were stretched by having to search through the authentic brochures to find the answers to the 'Chance' cards. During our school project, we, too, had started to realise that developing writing skills and teaching grammar could be part and parcel of the process of encouraging spontaneous interaction. Emer's project showed us how readily reading could also be integrated.

> • Look back to chapter 3. What other types of meaningful activity incorporating reading can be used?

Problems and lessons to be learned!

Case study 5: Teaching pupils with Special Educational Needs

The success of our school project and of the student teachers' projects was very encouraging. Nevertheless, we could not help wondering how feasible such projects were with more problematic groups. So we were delighted when **Eleanor Mayes** invited one of us to work with a group of fifteen Year 7 pupils, who had been designated as having a wide range of particularly demanding Special Educational Needs. The department in the large, mixed London comprehensive school had decided to teach these pupils in a small separate class. Thirteen of them were at Stage 2 or 3 with a reading age of about eight. They included Sally, who had hearing problems, Kerry and Kalee both with a visual impairment, Robert, Tyrone and Gary with behavioural problems, Mark and Barry with dyslexia, and several pupils who had just arrived in Britain. Two pupils, Claire and Eddie, were at Stage 5.

The topic was *Animals*. We decided that the aim of the problem-solving task would be to create an environmentally-friendly zoo. Pupils would start by placing cards on a bare zoo map to show where the cages, reptile house and pool should go, and then allocate the animals, according to which needed the most space and shade and so on. Photos taken on safari in Kenya were displayed to suggest the natural environment of wild animals. As a surprise element (and to cope with any violent disagreements!) pupils were to be given an envelope half-way through the exercise with extra fences in it in case the tigers had ended up next to the café! The zoos would then be displayed. We were aware that this problem-solving task reflected the classic problem of teaching pupils with SEN: in order to make it linguistically accessible, we had rendered it cognitively unchallenging. After all, it is fairly self-evident what are the optimum conditions for most animals. So to add a sense of genuine purposeful language use, we decided that pupils would cut up a photocopy of their zoos into a jigsaw puzzle that the other groups could play. As before, we would drip-feed in the SIL language that they would need.

In what way did we have to adapt our initial plans?

- First, it rapidly became clear that the language we had planned to teach was too complex. It had to be pruned down even more than in our previous project, sometimes even to single word utterances.

- More difficult to resolve was how to find a way of helping the pupils to work together collaboratively. We observed that they seemed to find it enormously difficult to relate to each other constructively. Many of the boys regularly entered the classroom and immediately began to cuss and fight each other, and some of the girls seemed to live in their own isolated worlds playing with fluffy toys they had brought in. Even when they did begin to communicate, our observations seemed very similar to those of another of the student teachers, Marie-Pierre Hamard. She noted from her project that the small group of low attainers in her class:

> have a confused approach to speaking. For example, A spoke but B did not react to A's sentence. She simply said something else, something that **she** wanted to say, regardless of what had just been said, so there were no real links in the conversation. There was also no real turn-taking since they often interrupted each other, those with strong personalities tending to impose their own views. Whereas the high attainers valued the discussion involved in coming to an agreement (the process itself), the low attainers valued only the result and completed the activity as quickly as possible. Somehow they failed to see the purpose of the interaction or even to understand the basic rules of conversation.

We had a similar problem on our hands with the whole of our Year 7 group!

> • In extract 7 of chapter 1, we saw that Canale described four components of communicative competence. Which one does the problem above relate to?

To tackle the problem, we decided:

• to structure the final activity more tightly, using an actual object (a dice) to determine both who should speak next and what they should say. So flashcards of the places in the zoo (cages, café, pool, etc.) would be placed on the board with numbers beneath them. Pupil A would roll the dice and then, according to the number shown, decide where to put that particular place on the map. A similar process would happen to place the animals;

• we had to build even more short bursts of pair work into preceding lessons than we had planned in order to get them used to working together;

• we had to institute a reward system not only for using SIL but also for sensible turn-taking. So we made a point of saying after each pair work activity not only who had done it well and giving out stickers, but exactly what it was that had made it so good. This inevitably meant using some English to make explicit what was involved in having a conversation. We hoped, however, that this would be justified since, over a longer period, pupils would develop these collaborative skills alongside the use of SIL. An activity like the French and Saunders video would also perhaps have been useful at the start of the project in enabling them to understand the nature and purpose of successful communication.

Table 4.4. Plan of lessons for Animals

Topic language	TP	PT	PP	Interaction language
1 Explanation of project Revision of animals	T mimes animal; Ps guess. T says *fenomenal* if pupil gets it right. T gets p to mime: *tu turno.* T deliberately does mime too fast to teach ps *problema? Repetid.*	Ps volunteer to mime, do it too fast, etc.	P1 mimes animal. P2 guesses. Pelmanism; matching pictures of animals to written words: *mi turno, tu turno, fenomenal.*	*Mi turno, tu turno. Repetid. Problema? Fenomenal.*
2 Places in zoo: *el estanque, la jaula, la casa de los reptiles*	T mouths places in zoo; pupils lipread. T does it too fast to revise *problema? Repetid.*		P1 mouths places. P2 lip reads.	*Mi turno, tu turno. Repetid.*

Cerca, lejos, aquí	T mimes. Ps guess.	Ps volunteer to mime.	P1 mimes, P2 guesses.	*Mi turno, tu turno. Repetid.*
3 *A los cocodrilos les gusta nadar/ comer turistas/ la sombra*	T mimes animal and action saying: *a los cocodrilos les gustan nadar.* Ps say phrase.	Ps volunteer to mime animal and action.	P1 mimes animal and action. P2 guesses.	*Mi turno, tu turno. Repetid.*
4 *A los cocodrilos les gusta nadar/ comer turistas/ la sombra*	T creates silly and sensible combinations by matching written cards in columns on the board under noun + likes + verb; e.g. asking ps: *a los peces les gusta volar. De acuerdo?*	Ps volunteer to make sentences.	Ps have similar cards to match up. Worksheet of posters for two zoos. Ps must decide which is most environmentally friendly.	*De acuerdo? Problema? Fenomenal.*
5 Revision of places, *cerca de, aquí*	T puts animals in 'silly' places in zoo, asking: *pon x aquí, cerca de la casa de los reptiles de acuerdo?* Listening activity: ps place animals according to instructions.	'Chinese whispers' in two teams; T gives 'silly' instructions e.g. put crocodiles near fish. Pupils pass it down line; last person has to place animal according to instruction.	Domino game. Card has picture of animal on one half and written word for place on another.	*Pon x aquí. De acuerdo. Mi turno, tu turno. Problema? Fenomenal.*
6 All topic language	T models making the zoo. Numbered flashcards of places on the board, along with basic zoo map. T rolls dice, asking ps *cuál luego?* Ps respond also saying where to place it. Numbered flashcards of animals on the board. T rolls dice, asking ps *cuál animal?* Ps respond saying where to place the animal.		Ps put places onto zoo map. Ps put animals onto map.	Spontaneous use of all SIL including *cuál animal, cuál luego?*

7 All topic language	T shows one half of animal and asks: *qué es?* Ps guess.		Ps. do jigsaw puzzles.	*Pon x aquí.* *De acuerdo?* *Qué es?*
8 All topic language			Poster to advertise environmentally-friendly zoo to be made using ICT.	

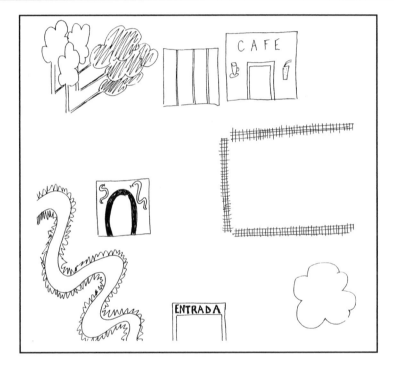

Figure 4.3. Zoo map used to practise the language

Teaching is a process of trial and error. It was only after the jigsaw activity that we realised that we should have cut up the puzzles ourselves. It is in fact quite a complex process to decide exactly how to create the puzzle so that there are just enough clues on each piece to be able to make a sensible guess but not so many as to make it too obvious. Pupils tended to cut up the jigsaw at random, so that each piece was either too hard or too easy to place. Hence perhaps one pupil's comment: *I liked making the zoo. I didn't like boing the jezor.* They did however engage enthusiastically in making the poster.

This was, as we had expected, the most challenging of classes to work with. Their lack of motivation, their sense of being failures was hard to combat in such a short period of time. Nevertheless, there were some small but promising signs of pupils beginning to internalise the language to the point that they could use it spontaneously in another context. Robert for example responded *Muy buen* when his partner guessed his mime correctly. Claire asked *problema?* when Sally was clearly struggling. And, as importantly, we felt that we had gained a clearer picture of some of the issues to consider when working with such pupils.

- Can you devise a more meaningful problem-solving activity to cover the topic of animals for a group of pupils with Special Educational Needs?
- What would be the interaction language that would need to be gradually drip-fed in?
- What else could be done to enable pupils to develop the necessary conversational,

Case Study 6: Overload!

The problem that emerged from the final project was not so much their level of motivation and attainment, since they were an enthusiastic Year 7 mixed ability group with some high-attaining pupils. It was more a question of mental overload, of making the task too challenging. Delphine Buforn also worked with Jane Darcy as her school-based tutor. The topics to be covered over a short period were *Time, Daily Routine* and *Clothes*. Delphine knew this was a good class and really wanted to stretch them and extend their competence. So she decided that they would play a board game, incorporating all three topics. When they landed on a square, pupils would pick up a card with a question on it, for example, about the time they got up in the morning, or what clothes they wore when. As a highly motivated and conscientious student, she was keen to add an additional sense of purpose to the game. So according to the response they gave, pupils would also build up their character profile, along the lines of magazine questionnaires. Finally, as she was also very interested in differentiation, pupils would play the game in attainment groups, each group having cards based on either simple or more extended topic language. So the class was asked to cope with:

- Language crossing a number of topic areas;
- A wide range of interaction language;
- A complex board game.

All in all, pupils did manage to use some phrases spontaneously despite these obstacles, the most popular of which were phrases such as *j'ai gagné* and *jette le dé*, which pupils remembered from a song with mimes that Delphine had composed especially for the project (Figure 4.4). Songs proved to be a highly effective means of inputting interaction language. There was perhaps a need, however, for more pair work in preceding lessons which would have enabled pupils to practise the language so that they could internalise it; to push them to interact with each other more before the final game playing session; drip-feeding rather than a lethal dosage!

Sung to the tune of *Alouette*

Qui commence? C'est à qui?
C'est à toi
C'est à toi
Qui commence? C'est à qui?
C'est à toi
Tu commences!

Sung to the tune of *10 Green Bottles*

Qu'est-ce qu'on doit faire?
C'est facile, jette le dé
avance de deux cases.
Vas-y, prends une carte,
ça suffit, stop, tu triches,
c'est à moi,
j'ai gagné

Figure 4.4. Songs to practise board game language

The amount of spontaneity achieved by Delphine's pupils was not as great as she had hoped. In her evaluation of the project, she makes some interesting observations which are of benefit to any of us about to embark on a similar project in the future. It relates to the question we raised in chapter 3 about matching the level of complexity of a task to pupils' competence and confidence. Delphine suggests that the main obstacle to spontaneity is mental overload, resulting in an inability to cope with the task in hand, which, in turn, lowers pupils' self confidence and forces them to resort to asking for help or speaking English. As Peter Skehan and Pauline Foster (1997) point out, there is only so much processing space in the brain. There simply is not room to produce the language spontaneously and fluently, if you are also having to cope with a complex task. Delphine felt that in future, at least when introducing the notion of SIL to pupils for the first time, she would be careful to ensure that:

- the problem-solving task or game was straightforward;
- the amount of topic language required was restricted;
- the amount of interaction language was limited;
- there was plenty of pair work practice of the interaction language.

Chapter 4 has offered some examples of carefully structured problem-solving tasks that match familiar GCSE topics and has suggested ways in which the interaction language needed to perform them can be taught alongside the topic language. Since it can be planned for and prepared in advance, this kind of approach is an important way of building up both the teacher's and the pupils' confidence in engaging in spontaneous use of the target language.

- The problem-solving tasks here were mostly aimed at beginner classes; Years 7 and 8. How could they be adapted for older classes to provide amongst other things a greater cognitive challenge, a richer content, drawing, for example, on some of the suggestions in chapter 3?

Before moving on to the final chapter, it may be worth reminding ourselves of the key lessons that we learned from the projects in this chapter:

* the power of language with a strong affective content;
* the power of the sound of words;
* the importance of genuinely meaningful language use for developing pupils' confidence and their listening skills;
* the way grammar teaching and the development of reading and writing skills can be integrated into encouraging spontaneous interaction;
* the need to restrict the cognitive and linguistic demands on pupils; to avoid mental overload;
* the need to provide adequate modelling and practice of each of the elements required for the final problem-solving task;
* the need to take into account pupils' personalities and learning styles, as well as their level of attainment;
* the need to make explicit what is involved in successful communication;
* the importance of trying to provide pupils with some choice about the language to be learned and opportunities to say what they want to say.

We will see all these themes emerge in the final chapter. But it also takes us one stage further. It moves us beyond the presentation and practice stage, beyond guided pair and group work towards the end of the continuum we referred to in chapter 3. To some extent, the tasks described in chapter 4 are contrived and rather limited, especially as they were aimed at younger pupils. Hopefully, they are meaningful and relevant but they are limited in terms of richness of content and the amount of say pupils had in what was to be learned and how. Chapter 5 offers another way of developing pupils' spontaneous use of the language; this time through the everyday business of a group of pupils and their teacher being in the classroom together. We will explore:

* how the teacher can be more flexible, moving outside the usual scheme of work, and responding to pupils' needs and interests as they arise and creating more opportunities for them to work independently;
* how everyday interaction in the classroom, like taking the register and setting homework, can be exploited;
* how this can be a powerful tool in developing pupils' grammatical understanding.

We will suggest that, although initially such an approach may appear too time-consuming, in the long term pupils are better equipped to face the demands not only of authentic communicative interaction but even the GCSE examination! Of course, such interaction cannot operate in a vacuum and we urgently need to review the content of modern languages lessons as Do Coyle and Kim Brown and Margot Brown, amongst others, advocate. Nevertheless, we will see how the classroom itself and the process of talking about how the language works and about how it is learned can be a rich source of spontaneous use of the target language.

Useful follow-up reading

Grenfell, M and Harris, V. (1999) *Modern languages and learning strategies; in theory and in practice.* London: Routledge. Chapter 4 has some ideas for ways of teaching turn-taking skills.

Page, B. (1992) *What do you mean it's wrong?* London: CILT. For an interesting discussion of how to tackle errors.

Brown, K and Brown, M. (1996) Pathfinder 27: *New Contexts for Modern Language Learning; Cross-curricular Approaches.* London: CILT. For a wide range of practical activities to make GCSE topics more meaningful.

Skehan, P. (1989) *Individual Differences in Second Language Learning.* London: Edward Arnold. For a discussion of the vast range of factors that may affect pupil performance.

5

Classroom routines and linguistic progression

Introduction: Exploring a dilemma

There are certain situations that arise in the modern languages classroom which are the subject of a lively discussion amongst practitioners as to whether L1 (the mother tongue) or L2 (the target language) is best employed; or indeed if the situations warrant any attention at all. These include:

- taking the register and dealing with late arrivals;
- the setting of homework;
- providing feedback on work;
- the setting of targets for the lesson;
- assessing whether the lesson targets have been met;
- pupils and teachers talking about and analysing grammar;
- dealing with messages and visitors to the classroom.

We invite you to explore two commonly-held and contrasting views.

View One

The first view revolves around the assumption that, since classroom learning time is so short and precious, the focus of attention must remain firmly riveted on the topic/content language; the situations, grammar and vocabulary directly related to a specific exam or scheme of work. As a result, the situations outlined above may be dealt with in English, either swiftly (register, late arrivals, etc.) or more at length (grammatical explanations, feedback, the setting of homework, etc.). The reasons given for such an approach are:

i   the L2 required is quite simply too complicated;
ii the use of L2 would be too time-consuming, thus detracting from getting through the syllabus and concentrating on exam/assessment-related issues;
iii the message is too important to risk possible misunderstanding.

View Two

The second view revolves around the assumption that it is vital that time be taken to plan for and exploit, through the medium of L2, the interaction stemming from such situations. To ignore their learning potential would be to disadvantage the learners or even contradict how language works as a system of communication. The reasons given for this approach are:

i   it is important to demonstrate that L2 is not so much the object of instruction, but rather a useful and exciting medium through which the learners can express themselves, and perhaps ultimately learn new concepts;

ii   the language inherent in such situations is often the language that produces the greatest spontaneity since it is a response to an immediate and real event;

iii greater variety is being brought into the learning process through avoidance of a repetitive diet of predominantly situational language based on topic areas that are almost in every sense foreign to the learners;

iv   there is often a vividness, emotional depth and intensity of experience associated with the language used in these situations which probably means it is safe to assume that the learners will retain the phrases encountered long after the flavours of different ice-creams and other such memorabilia from the GCSE-defined content have become a mere distant memory;

v   the situations being exploited are replete with useful structures and vocabulary that are easily transferable to a range of other contexts, both inside and outside the classroom. One of the dangers of the topic-bound GCSE syllabus is that pupils fail to make the connection that the *je voudrais* learned in the context of buying a drink in a café, for example, can also be used to buy a ticket at the railway station!

vi   the learners are better equipped to cope on their own; to take risks with the language, to negotiate meaning, to handle unpredictability, to overcome communicative road blocks, to make the language their own.

A dominant element of this debate is the simple question as to whether the game is really worth the candle. In other words, is the time dedicated to the setting up and exploitation of classroom situations rewarded richly enough in terms of the linguistic dividend that can be cashed out in the form of improved exam success? There may be some valuable spin-offs in terms of pupils being able to produce the language more spontaneously but is this at the expense of the grammatical accuracy required for the higher GCSE grades? It goes without saying that there are other equally important dimensions to this debate, not least the aims of modern language teaching itself. It is because this type of approach implies risk-taking not only by the pupils but also by the teacher, as he or she moves away from a familiar scheme of work, that we have placed it at the end of our book.

It is very difficult to capture on paper both the **process** by which everyday classroom routines can be exploited and the **outcomes** in terms of pupils' growing communicative competence. Despite these constraints, we propose diving into the classroom and observing, on the basis of transcriptions from one lesson, how this can happen.

This is a mixed ability Year 8 class of 26 pupils, who are almost half-way through their first year of learning French. The school is an urban 12–18 comprehensive school, in an area where the highest-attaining pupils go to the local grammar schools. The following extracts, although a snapshot of the start of just one lesson, are the outcome of regular 5–10 minute slots every lesson during which their teacher, James Stubbs, has exploited taking the register on a regular basis since the start of the year.

- As you read the extracts, you may find it useful to consider not only pupils' ability to produce the language spontaneously but also **what the teacher's grammatical agenda is.**

However, before encountering the class, we should perhaps first take a quick sidestep away from the classroom and briefly summarise the model of grammar teaching that we will be exploring in more depth throughout chapter 5. It will hopefully help to make sense both of the classroom extracts and also the overall shape of the chapter.

A model of grammar teaching

The teaching of grammar is clearly a highly complex, not to say controversial, issue. We have seen in chapter 1 the notion of two complementary sides to language learning:

Johnstone (extract 1)	intuitive, spontaneous	analytical, reflective
Skehan and Foster (extract 3)	fluency	accuracy

Our model draws on these two dimensions and, broadly speaking, moves along the continuum shown in Table 5.1.

Implicit understanding	⟶	Explicit knowledge
Unconscious, 'natural' language acquisition		**Conscious** language learning
Exposure to the language in a meaningful context. Pupils hear and then use the language without necessarily understanding how the grammar works. They practise and use the language as *unanalysed chunks*, as Rosamond Mitchell describes in chapter 1. Care is taken however to ensure that mime, games and songs highlight key features of the language, such as gender or verb endings. These act as a 'hook' on which to hang future grammatical exploration and explanation.	**Transference.** The unanalysed chunks are transferred to other contexts, to fulfil other communicative needs. This not only reinforces their communicative potential but also helps to raise pupils' grammatical awareness, to spot patterns in the language and to guess what the rules might be.	**Explanation.** Pupils use the target language to discuss the grammar of the target language. They identify what is/is not correct and explain why.

Table 5.1. A continuum of grammar teaching

Clearly, there is considerable overlap between the three stages and the teacher is constantly adapting what he or she is doing, both according to the pupils' responses and to the stage of development of a particular structure. At any one point, for example, he or she may simply be **exposing** pupils to the new structure A, whilst at the same time providing an opportunity for structure B to be **transferred** to a new context and also encouraging pupils to **explain** the rules governing structure C. This is another reason for placing this chapter at the end of the book. It is highly demanding for the teacher to keep track of where he or she is going with each structure! A further source of progression is within the routine itself; it can start off fairly simply with lots of visual support and become more and more complex and linguistically challenging. And finally the routines have to be embedded within the syllabus that pupils are following. The process, then, is not simply a linear one, where presentation and practice of a predictable area of topic language leads to production. It is much more of a patchwork, where topic language is interwoven with the language of the classroom, and where **implicit** understanding of one area of grammar may be running alongside the development of **explicit** knowledge of another.

The complexities of the process made it difficult to know how to structure the chapter, especially since we wanted to include lots of examples from the classroom, which automatically meant that a whole range of things was going on. We were back to the issue of progression that we confronted when designing the structure of the book itself! On the one hand, we could structure the sections of the chapter to reflect progression from the implicit to the explicit. Assuming that the explicit stage might perhaps be the most challenging for teachers, such a progression might also reflect moving from simple to more ambitious activities to experiment with. It was not as simple, however, as illustrating the progression by exploring the growth of just one structure over a number of lessons. We wanted also to show how the routine itself could become more and more linguistically demanding over time and to provide a range of different examples of classroom routines, different grammatical structures and in a number of languages. Table 5. 2 shows how we tried to reconcile these various strands of progression.

	Stage of grammatical awareness	Classroom context
Section 1	**Exposure** to different structures within **one** routine and **one** lesson; the present and past tenses and *on peut*.	The beginnings of a lesson; taking the register and warm-ups.
Section 2	**Transference** and progression **across routines.** How one of the expressions pupils were exposed to (*on peut*) can be developed through new contexts; six key principles for heightening grammatical awareness.	Pupils asking permission, e.g. to close the window, go to the toilet, play a game, etc.
Section 3	**Exposure** and progression within the **same routine over time**; from verbs to modals to time markers.	The main focus is on setting homework, although other classroom routines such as peer assessment and assessing the teacher's lesson are also briefly discussed.
Section 4	**Explanation.** Verb endings in the present tense.	Talking about how the language works.

Table 5. 2. The structure of chapter 5

We appreciate that the way we have defined progression within this chapter is as blunt and crude a tool as the division within the book itself between presentation, practice, guided production and classroom routines. Nevertheless, it hopefully provides one way of making sense of how classroom routines can be exploited to ensure both linguistic progression and spontaneous interaction. Now back to the classroom!

Section 1: Beginnings

- Exposure to the language
- Taking the register, dealing with late arrivals

Although the exposure stage relies heavily on the use of **unanalysed chunks** of language, James Stubbs ensures that the context in which the chunks are used is as memorable and meaningful as possible. Whilst he may simply be **exposing** pupils to the language, he also has his own **grammatical agenda**, in other words, they are aiming to sow the seeds to develop at a later stage pupils' awareness of how the language works.

So the chunk of language is provided with its own grammatical personality. Its salient features are stressed through sound, colour, gestures and the other multi-sensory devices, outlined in chapter 2 and illustrated in more detail in the next section.

Alongside trying to identify this agenda, you may also find yourself asking *exactly what is happening at this point in the routine?!* Since you cannot actually see the pupils, it can sometimes be quite hard to follow just from the interaction what is going on. For this reason, after each extract, a commentary is given, along with a brief explanation of the teacher's grammatical agenda.

Extract 1

T:	*Gareth?*	Gareth?
Class:	*Absent*	Absent
T:	*Absent?*	Absent?
Class:	*Non.*	No.
P:	*Il sèche.*	He's skiving.
T:	*Il sèche? Gareth … sèche?*	*Non.* He's skiving? Gareth … skiving. No.
Class:	*Si!*	Yes!
T:	*Non!*	No!
Class:	*Si!*	Yes!
Brian:	(words unclear)	
T:	*Pardon? Allez-y la classe; on dit Brian …*	Pardon? Go on, class; we say Brian …
Class:	*Brian, je n'ai pas entendu.*	Brian, I did not hear.
T:	*Alors, je n'ai pas entendu. Toute la classe …*	So, I did not hear. Everyone …
Class:	*Je n'ai pas entendu … veux-tu répéter, s'il te plaît.*	I did not hear … could you repeat please?
Brian:	*Gareth est avec Janine.*	Gareth is with Janine.
T:	*Gareth et Janine, ils sèchent … ensemble? Non!*	Gareth and Janine, they are skiving … together? No!
Class:	*Si!*	Yes!
T:	*Non!*	No!
Class:	*Si!*	Yes!

▨ Commentary

What is happening?

Within the general discussion of who is absent and why, a familiar contradiction routine swings into action about whether Gareth is skiving or not. Although at an early stage in their learning, pupils are given the opportunity to provide their own explanations and to disagree with the teacher. Brian bravely leaps to Gareth's defence, saying he is with Janine. He does this quite tentatively, however, thus prompting the teacher to exploit the use of a newly-emerging phrase *Je n'ai pas entendu*. This is linked automatically by the class to the phrase *Veux-tu répéter s'il te plaît* – a phrase that the class by now is using spontaneously without any teacher prompting.

What is the teacher's grammatical agenda?

There are several items here that are part of the teacher's on-going grammatical agenda. These are:

- past tense with *Je n'ai pas entendu* with mimes that stress the subject pronoun, the negative and the past participle of a *–re* verb.
- use of modals with *Veux-tu répéter, s'il te plaît,* with lots of stress on the second person singular aspect of *vouloir.*

Extract 2

The discussion continues as to Gareth and Janine's whereabouts.

T:	*Peut-être … quelles sont les autres possibilités? Et pourquoi est-ce que Janine est absente, pourquoi? Alors, qu'est-ce que vous pensez? D'autres possibilités? Karl?*	Perhaps … what are the other possibilities? And why is Janine absent, why? So, what do you think? Some other possibilities? Karl?
Karl:	*Elle est chez Monsieur Mendle.*	She is with Mr Mendle.
T:	*Elle est chez Monsieur Mendle? C'est probable ou possible?*	She is with Mr Mendle? Is that probable or possible?
Class:	*Probable.*	Probable.
T:	*Probable? Levez la main si vous pensez que c'est probable … et levez la main si vous pensez que c'est possible. Mmm … OK Samantha, qu'est-ce que tu penses?*	Probable? Put your hand up if you think that it is probable … put your hand up if you think that it is possible. Mmm … OK Samantha, what do you think?
P:	*Il est malade.*	He is ill.
T:	*Il est malade? Malade … oui … vous pensez? Levez la main si vous pensez que c'est probable … levez la main si vous pensez que c'est possible … levez la main si vous pensez que c'est impossible … levez la main si vous pensez qu'il sèche.*	He is ill? Ill … yes … you think so? Put your hand up if you think that it is probable … put your hand up if you think it is possible … put your hand up if you think that it is impossible … put your hand up if you think that he is skiving.
Class:	*Il sèche!*	He's skiving!

T:	*Non!*	No!
Class:	*Si!*	Yes!
T:	*Non!*	No!
Class:	*Si!*	Yes!
T:	*Peut-être. Neil, Lisa,* [continues with register] *la date?*	Perhaps. Neil, Lisa, [continues with register] the date?
Class:	*Le huit mars, deux mille.*	The 8th of March 2000.

Commentary

What is happening?

Here the teacher is working quite hard at prompting the pupils to think within the language by providing alternative suggestions as to where Gareth and Janine could be.

What is the teacher's grammatical agenda?

As well as ensuring that *il/elle* are used appropriately, he is setting in motion some very important 'future content' connected with the language of speculation. This is in the form of *probable/possible/impossible* and *Qu'est-ce que tu penses/vous pensez?* At present, this is very much at the listen-and-respond stage. The idea is just to sensitise the class to the whole concept of speculating where somebody could be and give them the freedom to come up with their own suggestions. What the teacher hopes to achieve in the much longer term within this routine is the use of the subjunctive, as an *unanalysed chunk*, after the phrases *probable/possible/impossible que.*

Where did the language come from?

At this point it might be reassuring to take another quick sidestep and explain how it is that the pupils are able to work within the language like this. The secret seems to lie in the provision of visual support coupled to the techniques for memorable drilling outlined in chapter 2.

Initially, the teacher brings the OHT (Figure 5.1) to each lesson to support pupils' comments. At first, pupils are just required to reply with *présent/présente*. In order to facilitate this distinction, all the boys are asked first, then all the girls. Special attention is given to stressing the *e* ending for the feminine form and that the *t* is pronounced. It may be, that, as part of this process, *absent/absente* is also exploited. The next time the register is undertaken the boys and girls are mixed up and care is taken to ensure that each answers with the appropriate adjective. Later still, reasons for absence are added in. During the process the teacher starts to raise grammatical awareness, leading to simple explanations such as:

T: *Quelle est la différence entre absent et absente?*

Class: *Absent pour un garçon. Absente pour une fille.*

Later still, this explanation may be extended to add in *parce que c'est féminin/masculin.*

As pupils gain familiarity with the routine and the language passes into their repertoire, the OHT can be withdrawn.

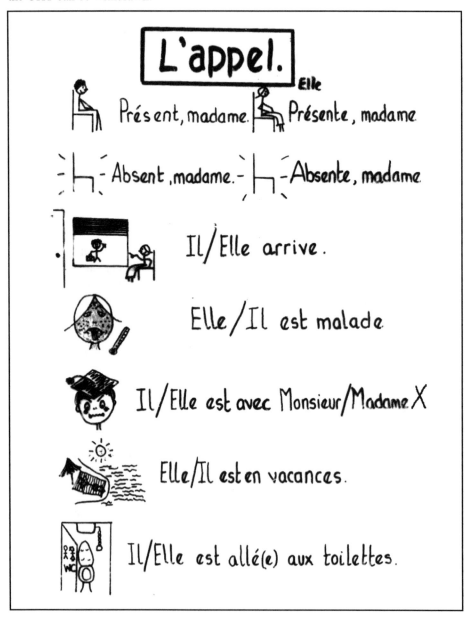

Figure 5.1. Visual support for register routine

In the next extract, the class is looking at the OHT in Figure 5.2 and trying to guess what excuse another missing pupil will give for being late. These are in fact two OHTs. The written words on the right are an overlay that can be withdrawn, as pupils become more familiar with the language.

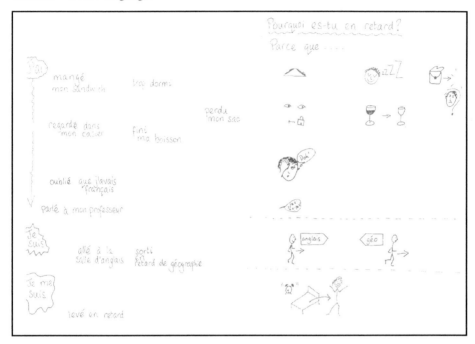

Figure 5.2. Visual support for lateness routine

Extract 3

T:	... Qu'est-ce que vous pensez? Il y a beaucoup de possibilités, alors ... qu'est-ce que vous pensez? Par exemple, 'pourquoi-est-elle en retard?' 'Parce qu' elle ...' Qu'est-ce qu'elle va dire? Elle va dire 'J'ai mangé mon sandwich'?	... What do you think? There are many possibilities, so ... what do you think? For example, 'why is she late?' 'Because she ...' What will she say? Will she say 'I ate my sandwich'?
Class:	Non.	No.
T:	Non? Non? 'J'ai oublié que j'avais français'? 'J'ai oublié que j'avais français', c'est possible? C'est possible? Oui? Non? Non? Peut-être une personne, une personne: 'pour-quoi-es-tu-en-re-tard?' C'est parce qu'elle a parlé avec un professeur? Oui? Un, deux, trois, quatre, cinq,	No? no? 'I forgot that I had French'? 'I forgot that I had French', is it possible? Is it possible? Yes? No? no? Perhaps one person, one person: 'Why-are-you-late?' It's because she spoke with a teacher? Yes? One, two, three, four, five, six, seven, eight, nine, ten ...

	six, sept, huit, neuf, dix ... ah! Plus que la majorité. Alors, qu'est-ce qu' elle va dire? 'Je suis en retard parce que j'ai trop dormi'? 'J'ai trop dormi'? Oui? Oui? ... 'Parce que j'ai fini ma boisson'? 'J'ai fini ma boisson.' Quelle boisson?	ah! More than half. So, what will she say? 'I am late because I overslept'? Yes? Yes? ... 'Because I finished my drink'? 'I finished my drink.' What drink?
Class:	*Du vin.*	Some wine.
T:	*Du vin. Du vin. Vin?! Du vin? Elle est alcoolique?!! C'est possible? Alors, c'est parce qu'elle a perdu son sac? C'est ça? ... oh la la! Toute la classe.*	Some wine. Some wine. Wine?! Some wine? She is an alcoholic?!! Is it possible? So, because she lost her bag? Is that right? Uh-oh!
Class:	*Pour-quoi-es-tu-en-re-tard?*	Why-are-you-late?
Natasha:	*Parce que je suis sortie en retard de géographie.*	Because I came out of geography late.
T:	*Ah! C'est acceptable?*	Ah! Is that acceptable?
Class:	*Oui/non.*	Yes/no.
T:	*A ta place, Natasha!*	Go to your seat, Natasha!
Class:	*Natasha, à ta place.*	Natasha, go to your seat.
T:	*A ta place. OK, assieds-toi. Ah! Alors, beaucoup de possibilités: 'j'ai mangé mon sandwich', 'j'ai trop dormi'...*	Go to your seat. OK, sit down. Ah! So, lots of possibilities: 'I ate my sandwich', 'I overslept'...

Commentary

What is happening?

Here we have the teacher continuing to build the speculation element into the lateness routine, but now also stressing the use of *parce que*.

There is also the well-established pattern of the class automatically launching into a *why-are-you-late?* question that is handled very well by Natasha, who provides an accurate stock response; an *unanalysed chunk*.

What is the teacher's grammatical agenda?

There is quite an intensive on-going grammatical agenda here with:

- use of the future tense with *aller* + infinitive in the guise of *Qu'est-ce qu'elle va dire?* Again, at this stage, and for this structure, the pupils simply have to listen and respond;

- stressing the possessive adjective *ta*;
- the use of a singular reflexive command in the form of *assieds-toi*;
- heavy emphasis by the teacher on the use of the past tense for what have until recently been present tense reasons for somebody being absent. In order to root the chunks of language even more firmly in their minds, they have sung several times the song on the OHT in Figure 5.3 to the tune of *The Animals went in Two by Two*.

Figure 5.3. Song for lateness routine

Extract 4

[... At last the class is in a position to ask to sit down ...]

P:	*Est-ce que la classe peut s'asseoir?*	Can the class sit down?
T:	*Ah! Toute la classe répétez: 'Monsieur Stubbs!'*	Ah! The whole class repeat: 'Mr Stubbs!'
Class:	*Monsieur Stubbs! Est-ce que la classe peut s'asseoir?*	Mr Stubbs! Can the class sit down?
T:	*Non* [... teacher mimes an activity]	No [... teacher mimes an activity that the class knows by now represents *Simon Says*]

Class: *Monsieur Stubbs! Est-ce que la classe peut jouer à Jacques a dit?*	Mr Stubbs can the class play *Simon says*?
T: *Oui.*	Yes.

Commentary

What is happening?

The regular routine is that pupils cannot sit down until the register has been taken. In the event, the teacher has decided that they were not out of the woods yet and sets up a requesting routine for a warm-up game, which turned out to be *Simon says*. In this lesson, it was cued by the teacher miming the activity but in other lessons pupils are invited to suggest the activity themselves, giving them some control over their own learning.

What is the teacher's grammatical agenda?

The teacher's grammatical agenda here is:

- a re-iteration of an **asking permission** routine involving *pouvoir* first with a reflexive verb *Est-ce que la classe peut s'asseoir?,* and then with *Est-ce que la classe peut jouer à Jacques a dit?*

This part of the lesson ended with the extract in section 9, chapter 2, on *Rewards and punishments*, where Matthew was given a forfeit for speaking in English.

Summary: where is the lesson?

At this point in time we possibly need to pause for breath and ask the question: Where is the lesson? With the register routine and the warm-up in the guise of the *Simon says* activity, ten minutes of lesson time have already elapsed without a single textbook page being turned or any topic area being exploited. Admittedly the pupils and the teacher have been communicating about a whole variety of issues, but to what end?

> - Re-read the transcriptions and jot down all the things that both impress and concern you about the interaction.

Commentary

If you are a 'View One' person then reading the above must have been quite a frustrating experience since you would have been continually wondering where the proper content of the lesson had got to. If you were a 'View Two' person, then you might possibly have been intrigued by what you read, but are wondering where all of the interaction is leading. It is probably safe to assume that most of us reside somewhere between these two extremes.

The class performance seems impressive on two counts. First of all, we have a mixed-ability class in its second term of French being exposed to and using spontaneously such language as **past tense phrases, present tense phrases, modal verbs, adjectives in the feminine and masculine form, appropriate subject pronouns,** *il ne faut pas +* **infinitive** (for Matthew's forfeit), and **question forms.** Secondly, there seems to be a wide range of strategies at play here; the ability to argue with and contradict the teacher, speculate, make suggestions and give reasons. Because of the narrowness of this one context, we could be excused for being sceptical, however. We might wonder perhaps if the pupils could be likened to a bunch of performing seals who, when given an appropriate stimulus, react in a particular way. Can the pupils move beyond the narrow confines of the interactions in the extracts? Can they start to unpack these unanalysed chunks of language so that they begin to understand how the language works and, as a result, start to operate independently? There is also the whole issue of topic/content language and where this fits into the overall learning pattern.

What happened to the content of the lesson?

The last point is easiest to deal with. At the current stage of writing the pupils have covered such topics as:

- personal information
- birthdays
- daily routine
- food
- celebrations (birthdays and Christmas)
- numbers 1–1000
- alphabet
- colours
- school (subjects, uniform and opinions)
- free time activities
- months, days of the week, seasons
- moods/feelings
- time.

Although the topic language is ever present and provides them with the vocabulary they need to move beyond the confines of the classroom, it plays more of a supporting than a leading role; it is not the mainspring of their linguistic development.

What happens to the grammar?

We would want to argue that the emphasis on the language arising from such classroom routines is proportionately much richer in structures than the more usual topic/content language. This fact alone means that grammar has got, on a statistical basis, a much greater chance of development.

Furthermore, as we shall see in the next section, the intensity and variety of contexts across which a single structure is used, together with a range of devices to promote grammatical understanding, make a powerful contribution to it being used with ever increasing understanding as a communicative instrument. A recent, successful OFSTED inspection of the modern languages department notes that:

> *Standards in work seen at the end of Key Stage 3 were much higher than those recorded in the 1999 Statutory Teacher Assessments. The majority of pupils were working at levels above the national expectation. They could engage in fairly long conversations on familiar topics and play the role of the teacher, posing questions and eliciting replies from the class. They could also seek information, ask for clarification, give reasons for actions and express personal opinions. Additionally, many pupils of higher ability at Key Stage 3 achieved very high standards, especially in listening and speaking. They could, for example, cope with unpredictable language in unexpected situations, discuss aspects of grammar and usage, negotiate deadlines for homework and even be humorous!*

The comments on Key Stage 4 were equally positive. But all you have been provided with so far is a snapshot from one lesson. There is with little indication as to how the phrases are going to be developed in the future. How are they going to be transferred to new contexts, so that pupils' grammatical awareness is heightened and they are not simply responding like the performing seals mentioned earlier?

Section 2: Transference

- Asking permission
- Six key principles for heightening grammatical awareness

In an attempt to illustrate how pupils' grammatical awareness can be encouraged, even at this early stage, we shall examine in depth the development of one structure: *pouvoir*. We have seen that it was one of the items on the teacher's grammatical agenda in the register and warm-up routine, with pupils asking *on peut s'asseoir/jouer à Jacques a dit?*

The whole process can be described using images relating to the birth of a structure and its future growth and development.

The structure is born within a specific context. However, in order to grow and develop in the pupils' minds, it needs to be nurtured through its early development across a **range of contexts.** These not only reinforce its communicative potential but also help the pupils to unravel **the**

grammatical facts of life. So it is given time to grow and explore the world outside before finally leaving home to live an extended and full life.

 Pupils thus become more independent both in terms of being freed up from the context-embedded nature of the situation in which they were first **exposed** to the language and in terms of much more insightful use of the language from a grammatical point of view.

There are six key principles that can help us in this process. These are listed below.

Birth, growth and development of the structure: *Je peux …?*

Principle 1: Know where you are going.

Knowing where you are going entails having an appropriate phrase and context in mind into which the structure *Je peux …?* can initially be embedded. Here the phrase *Est-ce que je peux être volontaire?* is suggested because there is often a strong desire amongst the pupils to ask to be a volunteer. Often these activities will be something as banal as handing out pieces of paper. If we neglect to exploit such situations linguistically, then we risk squandering one of the most important learning resources in the classroom: the human desire to want to do something. However, a situation has to be engineered in which there is a need, want and desire to use this particular phrase.

Principle 2: Engineer an appropriate situation.

This quite simply means putting pupils in a position where they want something, but, in order to do it, French has to be used. Because the power of the context is so clear, all the teacher has to do is spring in with the appropriate phrase to service the pupils' pressing linguistic need. So, for example, in the case of *Est-ce que je peux être volontaire?*:

- the teacher asks for a volunteer and receives lots of hands in the air with the pupils calling out 'Miss' or 'Sir';
- in the initial stages, the teacher might simply exploit *Moi, s'il vous plaît.* Alternatively he or she may proceed directly to the use of *Est-ce que je peux être volontaire?*

If he or she decides to proceed directly to the use of *Est-ce que je peux être volontaire?*, then it is helpful to follow another key principle that entails drilling the phrase in such a way that the class starts to feel confident with it in terms of fluency and pronunciation.

Principle 3: Exploit the phrase with intensity and depth on a whole-class basis.

Although many pupils may want to be volunteers, and indeed ultimately one pupil is going to ask to be a volunteer, we usually start by taking the pressure off individual pupils and exploiting *Est-ce que je peux être volontaire?* on a whole class basis. This makes the languages classroom a far less intimidating linguistic environment. The whole class repetition of the phrase involves the provision of appropriate visual support and the practice of the phrase in a memorable way, similar to the phrase *C'est quoi en français Chemistry?* in chapter 2. James Stubbs models the following and then encourages pupils to do the same:

- draws an *S* in the air to convey the sound of *Est-ce que*;
- for *je peux,* the pupils point at themselves to convey the meaning of *je* and then clasp their hands together as if pleading;
- for *être volontaire?* the pupils jump up and put a hand up as if they were excitedly volunteering to do something.

This not only stresses the salient grammatical features of a chunk of language (its grammatical personality), but also enables the pupils to feel confident in its use in terms of their ability to pronounce it fluently, quickly, accurately and quasi-spontaneously. At this particular juncture, they may not be able to say explicitly what is happening grammatically to the chunk of language, but they are certainly able to take the language and use it for themselves when appropriate.

Once the phrase has been practised appropriately and the teacher is confident that the class can pronounce it sufficiently well, he or she can return to the pupil who originally wanted to volunteer and see if they can manage the phrase on their own. However, the teacher does not expect that the pupils will retain this phrase effortlessly in the next lesson. This fact brings us on to the next important principle.

Principle 4: The nurturing of a phrase.

The steps outlined in **Principles 1–3** may need to be repeated on several future occasions until most members of the class are starting to use the phrase with ease. Then the phrase, or in this instance part of it, can be transferred into other contexts. This stage brings us on to our next principle.

Principle 5: Transfer to other contexts.

If we pursue the images of birth and nurture above, then this is the point in time at which our phrase is sent out into the world to experience new situations across a variety of contexts. Other particularly powerful contexts in which *Est-ce que je peux?* can occur are:

- *Est-ce que je peux avoir un point?* as part of an on-going team competition;
- *Est-ce que je peux chronométrer?/faire l'appel?* as part of a timing the register routine (see below);
- *Est-ce que je peux cacher la carotte/sortir?* as part of a *am I getting hot/cold?* game that the pupils particularly like playing. One pupil leaves the classroom. The class

decides where to hide the object and the pupil returns. The class counts from 1–100, getting louder if the pupil is close to the object and softer if they move away from it.

As the number of contexts grows, so does the difficulty in remembering the vocabulary and structures that can accompany the key structure *Je peux?* In order to help retention, the teacher can use songs as well as the visual support. The song below, which is sung to the tune of the Can-Can, also allows us to gain a glimpse into the range of contexts across which James Stubbs' Year 8 French class is starting to develop the use of the phrase *Est-ce que je peux?*

Est-ce que je peux   entrer dans la salle de classe
m'asseoir?
aller aux toilettes?

Est-ce que je peux   fermer la fenêtre parce que j'ai froid?
travailler avec lui ou elle?

As yet, we have been limiting ourselves just to the **first person singular** of *pouvoir*. If our phrase is going to survive in an ever-changing linguistic environment, then it needs to be able to adapt and change according to context. In the case of a verb, this means being able to exploit fully the different subject pronouns. This point brings us on to our last principle.

Principle 6: Allowing the phrase to live a full and extended life.

If the verb *pouvoir* is going to grow to its full potential, then progression must take place. This means not only transferring the chunk of language into other contexts, but also exploiting it using different persons of the verb, so that pupils are not limited to the first and second person singular Question and Answer routines, described by Rosamond Mitchell in extract 2 of chapter 1.

From **je peux** *... to* **la classe peut** *...?*

In a sense, in the extract from the one lesson, we came across *pouvoir* when it was halfway through its development. The OHT in Figure 5.4. shows how James Stubbs had already supported pupils in transferring *je peux* into the third person singular, so that they could ask, when he had finished taking the register, *La classe peut s'asseoir/jouer à Jacques a dit?* Giving pupils some choice over what games are to be played automatically provokes spontaneous use of the language. Because this transparency does not have to rhyme like the song does, it has been carefully categorised from a grammatical point of view with *er* and *ir* verbs grouped together.

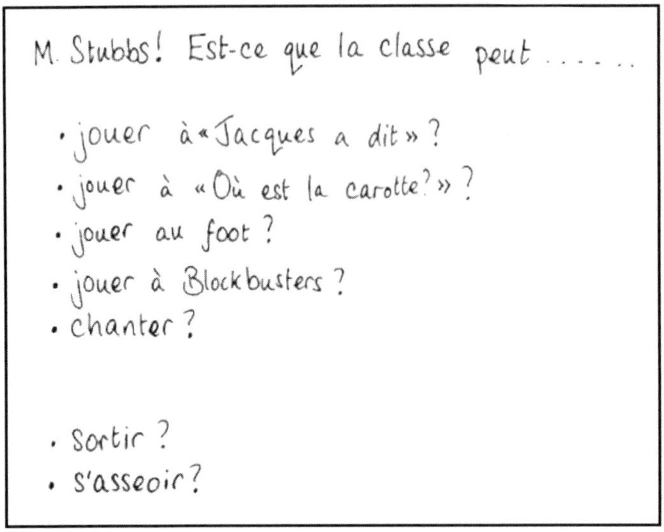

M. Stubbs! Est-ce que la classe peut . . . . . .

- jouer à « Jacques a dit » ?
- jouer à « Où est la carotte ? » ?
- jouer au foot ?
- jouer à Blockbusters ?
- chanter ?

- Sortir ?
- s'asseoir ?

Figure 5.4. Visual support for extending pouvoir

Extending pouvoir *to* nous pouvons/ ils peuvent

A team competition is a very powerful context for the exploitation of other subject pronouns. For example, if a team thinks it deserves a point, then it has to say *Est-ce que nous pouvons avoir un point, s'il vous plaît?* A discussion can then ensue as to whether they can or cannot have a point, thus producing *oui ils/elles peuvent avoir un point* or *non, oui ils/elles ne peuvent pas avoir un point.* The same discussion can also take place if an individual asks for a point, thus producing the language *oui, il/elle peut avoir un point* and *non, il/elle ne peut pas avoir un point.* With a slight change of emphasis, *tu/vous* can easily be employed when talking directly to an individual or a team concerning whether they can get points or not. The whole issue of discussing the awarding of points can lead on later into giving justifications, producing such language as *elle peut avoir un point parce qu'elle a dit* ... and even at a much more advanced stage to something like *elle ne peut pas avoir un point parce qu'elle aurait dû dire, à mon avis, ... et pas* ... (see section 4).

This kind of progression means that when it comes to the explicit exploration of the concept of a verb paradigm, then pupils have a very strong sense of subject pronouns, since they will all have been used in context, with very powerful mimes indicating whether it was he/she/they, etc. who is/are undertaking the action. Furthermore, we also have an example of a modal working with an infinitive. Once this fact is made more explicit, then we have the paradigm for all modals. It is only a small step from here to saying that *vouloir fonctionne comme pouvoir.*

It will not be possible to illustrate in such detail this kind of progression for all the structures in each of the various other classroom routines described. Nevertheless, these six principles are part and parcel of building up the pupils' confidence and independence both in using the language spontaneously and in understanding how it works.

> • James Stubbs exploits the register routine through a number of other activities. In Table 5.3. under *Language involved*, we list the language that his class actually used. How could you build up to it gradually, using the six principles and some of the activities discussed in chapter 2? You may want to come back to your original ideas, when you have read the rest of this chapter.

Activity	Language involved
Pupils requesting to take the register and time how long it takes.	*Est-ce que je peux faire l'appel, s'il vous plaît?* *Est-ce que je peux chronométrer, s'il vous plaît?*
Discussions in pairs as to how long the register routine took last time.	*La dernière fois c'était combien de secondes? Bon alors, je pense que c'était 54 secondes. Qu'est-ce que tu penses?*
Discussion in pairs as to how long it will take this time.	*Ça va prendre combien de secondes aujourd'hui? Qu'est-ce que tu penses?*
Discussion with a partner as to who won.	*C'était 50 secondes. Donc j'ai gagné parce que j'ai bien deviné. Un point pour moi.*
An evaluation of the routine in terms of its speed compared with last time and how well it was done.	*C'était plus/moins rapide.* *C'était bien/nul.*
The class being kept on its toes by the teacher sometimes entering wrong times on the OHT that he regularly uses for recording the time of the register or a false record of whether the pupils thought it had been done well or not.	*Monsieur, vous vous êtes trompé parce que c'était 50 secondes et vous avez écrit 51!* *Ça ne va pas!* *Monsieur, vous vous êtes trompé parce que nous avons dit 'bien' et vous avez écrit 'nul'.* *Ça ne va pas!*

Table 5.3. Exploiting the register routine

Although it might make sense to go straight on now to explore how pupils' growing understanding of the different uses of *pouvoir* could be made explicit, it may also be useful to explore the potential value of other classroom routines, apart from taking the register and asking permission. In the example of the growth of *pouvoir*, we were looking at progression **across** a range of contexts. In the examples in section 3, we will focus on progression **within** one context; the setting of homework.

Section 3: Other classroom routines

- Homework
- Peer assessment
- Assessing the teacher's lesson

Setting homework

For understandable reasons, the setting of homework is often regarded by teachers as an area of classroom interaction that is too important to risk doing in L2. Such an approach carries with it, however, the implicit message that if something is important, then it is said in English, which may devalue and undermine the position of L2 in the classroom. Equally important from the perspective of the debate here is the fact that, like taking the register, situations such as these are replete with useful structures and vocabulary that represent a rich new harvest in terms of the potential for linguistic progression. The examples that follow come from a Year 10 beginners' class spanning a time period of approximately eight months. The intention is to show how a homework routine can be gradually developed so that it becomes more and more complex and demanding linguistically.

Step 1

The whole process of helping the class to become familiar with the setting of homework in the target language began with the regular use of a standard OHT (Figure 5.5). This initially just carried the basic information required to understand what the homework entailed and when it was to be handed in.

Figure 5.5. Visual support for setting homework

A typical example looked like this:

Hausaufgaben:	Homework:
Was:	What:
1. *Das Alphabet lernen, bis es perfekt ist!* _____ *Sekunden.*	1 Learn the alphabet until it is perfect! _____ seconds.
2. *Die Nummern von 1 bis 100 lernen.*	2. Learn the numbers from 1 to 100.
3. *Die Fragen und Antworten zu:* *Vornamen/Nachnamen* *Wohnort* *Alter*	3. The questions and answers to: Forename/surname Place of residence (address) Age
Lernen! Test – schriftlich!	Learn! Test – written!
Für: Montag, den 17. Oktober	For: Monday the 17th of October

Prior to setting this homework, a negotiation process had taken place. It involved the teacher seeing how quickly he could say the alphabet. His attempt was timed by the class and then used as a bargaining point for setting the number of seconds in which the alphabet, set for homework, had to be said by the class itself at the start of the following lesson. The process of negotiation allowed pupils some limited control over their homework and generated a wealth of emotions!

The class was also asked to learn the numbers from 1–100. They had been working on this already and the homework was intended to prepare them for a test the following week. The test would also include the production of questions based on the sorts of key words found on forms in Germany.

In order to make sure the class was attentive and fully involved in the setting of homework, there was not only the negotiation about the alphabet. The teacher also used a standard technique with which the class was becoming familiar of slowly revealing the homework instructions on the OHT and getting the class to speculate on the key words in the explanation, e.g. *Montag, 17. Oktober, lernen, von … bis … , Fragen, Antworten, Test – schriftlich.* The usual strategies of awarding points for pupils who guessed the correct missing words was employed. At the end, the teacher recapped on the homework and got the class to put in, often with appropriate mimes, the missing words. This ensured that it was understood by everyone. It was then recorded in German in a homework diary; pupils, if they wished, providing an English summary of what was required.

Step 2

The class had been working intensively on the genders *der* and *die*, using the kinds of activities outlined in more detail in the next section. The work had been supported by the use of colour on the OHT and *gender walls*, pictures of *der* words on one wall and *die* words on the other.

Hausaufgaben für Montag, den 14. November:	Homework for Monday the 14th of November:
Die Gebäude lernen – der und die.	Learn the buildings – (genders).
Du musst die Gebäude innerhalb von _____ Sekunden sagen UND am Mittwoch, dem 16. November wird es einen schriftlichen Test geben, und zwar für alle Gebäude! – der/die/das	You must say the buildings within _____ seconds AND there will be a written test on Wednesday the 16th of November, namely on all the buildings! – (genders)

The general explanation for the homework has become slightly more complicated with the use of *du musst ... sagen* (rather than a simple infinitive, like *lernen*, for the instruction). Similarly, the explanation of the written test has proceeded from *Test – schriftlich!* to the entry involving the future tense.

Step 3

This next homework was a further linguistic departure since clear time markers (such as *first, then*) were employed to enable pupils to begin to string sentences together. Each of the markers had a specific mime associated with it. This particular class reacted very well to this approach and there was clear evidence of the use of such markers in other contexts, especially within their written work and when they were required to give quite long oral explanations.

An extra dimension has also been added to corrections, so that pupils must now explain **why** the mistakes were wrong. How they reached this level of grammatical awareness will also be discussed in the next section.

Hausaufgaben für Donnerstag, den 24. November:	*Homework for Thursday 24th November:*
Erstens: eine Zeitschrift oder eine Zeitung finden.	Firstly: find a magazine or a newspaper.
Dann: mindestens 4 kleine Fotos auschneiden.	Then: cut out at least 4 small photos.
Danach: eine Fantasiefamilie beschreiben.	After that: describe an imaginary family.
Und dann: Verbesserungen machen! Zum Beispiel:	And then: do corrections! For example:
Das postamt (x 5) – das Postamt, das Postamt, das Postamt,	The post office (x 5)
Das P ist groß, weil Postamt ein Substantiv ist. Ein Substantiv ist ein Ding, eine Person, ein Tier, ein Konzept oder ein Ort.	It's a capital 'P' because post office is a noun. A noun is a thing, a person, an animal, a concept or a place.

Step 4

In this final homework example, because the class had not as yet explicitly formulated the rules for reflexive verbs, no explanation for the corrections was required. An unusual and perhaps somewhat controversial dimension was that the class had to undertake translations in preparation for the Mastermind game. But these were translations with a difference, since the pupils had a powerful sense of audience; and their audience was their fellow pupils to whom they would be giving their sentences to translate, once they had been corrected by the teacher. This proved to be a hugely popular activity with lots of language being generated in terms of comments on each other's performance, etc. It tapped into a natural desire in the classroom to have some control over the nature of the tasks set and to communicate about such issues as feedback on work, marks, etc.

Hausaufgaben für Montag, den 22. Mai:	*Homework for Monday 22nd May:*
1. *Erstens das Testpapier ins Heft kleben.*	1 Firstly, stick the test paper into your exercise book.
2. *Zweitens <u>alle</u> Verbesserungen machen. z.B. Ich ziehe uns an. – Ich ziehe <u>mich</u> an. (x 5): Testverbesserungen x 5 machen.*	2 Secondly, do <u>all</u> the corrections. E.g. I get ourselves dressed. – I get <u>myself</u> dressed. (x 5) Do test corrections x 5.
3. *Drittens die Sätze für Mastermind vorbereiten. Das Thema ist ‚die Tagesroutine' – Präsens. Überschrift: Wie heißt folgendes auf Deutsch? Wie sagt man folgendes auf Deutsch?* *a Then they go downstairs and drink tea. (Dann gehen sie nach unten und trinken Tee.)* *b We are getting changed. (Wir ziehen uns um.)* *c They get dressed in the bathroom. (Sie ziehen sich im Badezimmer an.)*	3. Thirdly, prepare the sentences for Mastermind. The topic is 'daily routine'. Present tense. Title: What is the German for the following? How do you say the following in German?
Ihr müsst ein Minimum von 10 Sätzen schreiben.	You must write at least 10 sentences.
4. *Schließlich, die Sätze für eure strategische Kompetenz <u>üben</u> und <u>lernen</u>.* *Was musst du machen?* *– Erstens muss ich ...* *– Zweitens muss ich ...*	4. Finally, <u>practise</u> and <u>learn</u> the sentences for your strategic competence. What do you have to do? – Firstly, I have to ... – Secondly, I have to ...

By now the teacher had decided that he would not check himself that pupils had understood what were the first, second and third tasks connected with homework. Instead it was handed over to the pupils themselves, using the language listed under *strategic competence*. The class very much enjoyed extracting from their friends what exactly it was they had to do for homework and it also reinforced the whole feel for subject–verb inversion within the German language.

We have seen a number of strands of linguistic progression in this series of homeworks;

- from the use of infinitives for instructions (*lernen*) to the use of *modals (du musst ... sagen)*;
- from simple lists to time markers (*zuerst, danach, schließlich*);
- from usual word order to inversion of subject and verb;
- from the teacher determining the exact nature of the tasks to pupils having some say in it;

- from the teacher checking that pupils understood the homework to pupils testing each other.

> - Think of some of the usual types of homework that you regularly set your classes. Then fill in the table below suggesting how the language involved could gradually be made more complex and the pupils given more control over the tasks. Page (1992), for example, includes ideas like giving pupils a list of possible homework tasks from which they choose.

Homework	Step 1	Step 2	Step 3

Similar steps from the most simple ways of exploiting a routine to the more demanding can be used in both peer and teacher assessment. The next section does not illustrate them in such detail, however. It simply suggests possible starting points.

Peer assessment

The advent of the National Curriculum, OFSTED inspections and the league tables has meant that teachers are all too familiar with assessing pupils' work. It is less common, however, to find pupils being invited to comment on each other's performance. Yet this has a number of advantages:

- it helps to make the criteria by which they will be assessed more explicit;
- it moves assessment from being something subjective and personal to do with the

teacher's possible preferences to a more common set of objective standards;

- like the other routines, it provides a wealth of potentially useful and transferable language;
- it is fun!

For the sake of brevity and clarity, the two examples below represent a sample of the language employed in the same Year 10 class within the context of peer assessment. The first example is from the first week of the pupils' learning. The second is from the end of the year.

Example 1

Pupils had to say the numbers according to their partner's instructions. Although very little progress has been made in terms of the traditional content language (numbers)

P1. *Also, 1 bis 5. Los!*	A. So, 1 to 5. Go!
P2. *1,2,3,4,5.*	B. 1,2,3,4,5
P1. *Also, nochmal und …*	A. Okay, once again and …
Schneller!/langsamer!	Faster/slower!
Lauter!/leiser!	Louder/quieter!
Und nochmal …	And once again …
Stop! Das war …	Stop! That was …
Ganz toll	Really super
Gut	Good
Sehr schlecht	Very bad
Furchtbar	Awful

progress has been made in terms of the ability to communicate with one another and, more specifically, to begin to pass comments on their partner's performance.

An alternative is to make pupils' pronunciation the focus of their partner's comments.

Example 2

The next example exploits linguistically the natural curiosity that pupils have when work is handed back. In essence, they are allowed to yell at anybody in the room to find out how they got on in the test … provided it is in German!

Die Testergebnisse

P1. Hallo! Gary! Wieviele Punkte hast du für Kommunikation bekommen?

P2. Also, ich habe ____ Punkte für Kommunikation bekommen.

P1. Ach so! Das ist (ausgezeichnet ➝ wahnsinnig schlecht). Wie viele Punkte hast du für Grammatik bekommen?

P2. Also, ich habe ____ Punkte bekommen.

P1. Ach so! Das war nicht so gut wie die Kommunikation. Das ist nur _____ . Du musst: mehr üben/besser lernen/deine Verbesserungen machen!

Test results

P1. Oi! Gary! How many points did you get for communication?

P2. Well, I got ____ points for communication.

P1. I see. That is (excellent ➝ really bad). How many points did you get for grammar?

P2. Well, I got ____ points.

P1. I see. That wasn't as good as communication. That is only ____ . You have to: practise more/revise better/do your corrections!

Assessing the lesson

What pupils often find even more appealing than assessing each other's performance is to pass comment on the teacher's teaching. The OHT in Figure 5.6 is a standard transparency used by student teachers for starting to elicit comments on their lessons. The pupils are encouraged to argue with the teacher, who begins by asking:

T   Wie war die Stunde? Was meinst du? Es war toll, oder …?
Ps Nein, es war langweilig.

Pupils then discuss the lesson with each other.

***	Es war toll/unheimlich gut
**	Es war gut
*	Es war ziemlich gut/solala
–	Es war langweilig
– –	Es war schrecklich/furchtbar

Figure 5.6. Visual support for assessing a lesson

Summary

The last three sections have explored a range of everyday classroom situations in which pupils can be exposed to the meaningful use of language. Even though they initially use phrases as *unanalysed chunks*, we have seen how even at this stage, their awareness of the underlying grammar rules can be heightened by:

- multi-sensory drilling, which provides hooks on which they can later hang a more explicit grammatical knowledge;
- transference and progression across a range of contexts (*pouvoir*);
- progression within any one context (homework).

We have also seen ways in which they can be provided with opportunities to have some say, however limited, in the tasks set.

In the final section of the book, we explore the last stage, where pupils' growing understanding is made explicit. We will see how, even within this stage, there are a number of gradual steps that can be taken.

- Look back to Sue's letter at the end of chapter 1. Which words and phrases do you think were born in the classroom routines described in this section?

Section 4: Explanation

- From implicit to explicit knowledge
- Talking about how the language works

If we refer back to the View One/View Two dichotomy at the start of this chapter, then it is probably fair to suggest that the area where many teachers feel least comfortable in using the target language is the teaching of grammar. So, getting the pupils to use it to discuss how the language works may seem like an impossible hurdle. The purpose of this section is to suggest that getting pupils to talk about grammar through L2:

- is not only relatively easy, but also yields a massive linguistic dividend in terms of structural progression;
- fosters highly useful strategic competence related skills such as asking for/giving explanations, giving reasons and asking for clarification.

Furthermore, puzzling out how language works grammatically is not only great fun and cognitively challenging for many pupils, but also provides one of the few real communicative contexts within the modern languages classroom.

Let us take as an example how pupils might begin to unpack *Was meinst du?* (What do you think?), so that they can understand and explain the various verb endings in the present tense and begin to ask about and express opinions. Figure 5.7 summarises some of the activities already discussed in relation to *pouvoir* that might have been used in the initial *exposure* stage. As we have seen, it is during these stages that the grammatical personality of a phrase is stressed very heavily. In the phrase *Was meinst du?* two key grammatical features are stressed; the verb ending and the subject pronoun. The stressing of these salient grammatical points serves as a peg on which to hang further grammatical exploration and explanation.

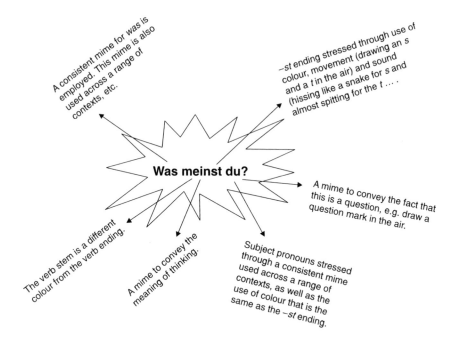

*Figure 5.7. Making '*Was meinst du?*' memorable*

Just like with *pouvoir,* the **transference** stage might have included a range of contexts and verb endings which encouraged pupils to ask about and express what they thought. For example, *what do you think about the homework, about the lesson, about your partner's test results?* The *–e* ending for the first person singular is stressed by the class bending forward at the waist by about 90° while simultaneously exaggerating the sound.

The final stage of making their increased awareness explicit can be subdivided into three distinct steps, expressed diagrammatically in Table 5.4. For ease of reference, stage 1 incorporates both the **exposure** and **transference** stages, since the focus for the rest of this chapter is stages 2–4 of the process.

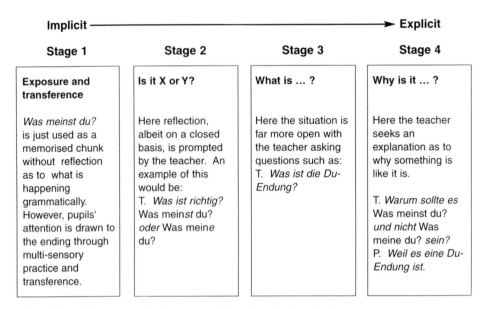

Implicit ──────────────────────────────────────→ **Explicit**

Stage 1	Stage 2	Stage 3	Stage 4
Exposure and transference	**Is it X or Y?**	**What is ... ?**	**Why is it ... ?**
Was meinst du? is just used as a memorised chunk without reflection as to what is happening grammatically. However, pupils' attention is drawn to the ending through multi-sensory practice and transference.	Here reflection, albeit on a closed basis, is prompted by the teacher. An example of this would be: T. *Was ist richtig? Was meinst du? oder Was meine du?*	Here the situation is far more open with the teacher asking questions such as: T. *Was ist die Du-Endung?*	Here the teacher seeks an explanation as to why something is like it is. T. *Warum sollte es Was meinst du? und nicht Was meine du? sein?* P. *Weil es eine Du-Endung ist.*

Table 5.4. Raising grammatical awareness through guided exploration

Stage 2: Is it X or Y?

Although the techniques described below are closed, future language is being sown for a more open response. The use of the metalinguistic term *Endung*/ending is particularly helpful in this respect. All the examples lend themselves to follow-up **partner work**.

Right or wrong?

T. *Was meine du?* Ist das richtig oder falsch?	*Was meine du?* Is that right or wrong?
C. Das ist falsch.	That is wrong.
T. *Was meinen du?*	*Was meinen du?*
C Das ist falsch.	That is wrong.
T. *Was meinst du?*	*Was meinst du?*
C. Endlich! Das ist richtig!	At last! That is right!

Black or green?

Quickly cover up an OHT with the verb paradigm on it and then quiz the class about the colour coding; perhaps the verb stem is in black and the endings are in green. Although the term *verb* is used in the dialogue below, it is not assumed the class actually understands what a verb is; they are simply being **exposed** to it. However, it is expected that they understand they are being asked about the rest of the word, hence the use of the word *Rest*.

T. Welche Farbe hatte die Du-Endung? War das –*st* grün oder schwarz?

What was the colour of the *Du* ending? Was –*st* green or black?

P. Also, das war grün, denke ich.

Erh that was green, I think.

T. Welche Farbe hatte der Rest des Verbs?

What was the colour of the rest of the verb?

P. Schwarz.

Black.

Is the ending X or Y?

T. Ist es *Was meinst du?* oder *Was meine du?* Was ist richtig? Ist es –*st du* oder –*e du?* Was ist die richtige Endung? Also mit dem Partner spekulieren. Den Partner fragen: Ist es *Was meinst du?* oder *Was meine du?* Was ist richtig?

Is it Was meinst du? or *Was meine du?* What is correct? Is it –*st du* or –*e du*? What is the correct ending? O.K. speculate on that with your partner. Ask your partner: Is it *Was meinst du* or *Was meine du?* What is correct?

Stage 3: What is …?

These examples are slightly more open in that alternatives are no longer given. Pupils are required to provide the information themselves without the linguistic support of the type given by the teacher above.

Mime and say

The teacher says the phrase but leaves out the –*st* ending, replacing it with the mime that was employed to emphasise the ending. Mime is also used for the personal pronoun *Du*. The class has to say what the missing ending and pronoun are.

T. *Was mein - -* [… teacher mimes the ending and the pronoun in the air …] *Was ist die richtige Endung?*

Was mein - - [… teacher mimes the ending and the pronoun in the air …] What is the correct ending?

C. *Es ist +* class mimes and says missing ending and pronoun.

It is + class mimes and says missing ending and pronoun.

Mouth and say

This is basically the same approach, but the missing ending and personal pronoun are not mimed but mouthed.

What have I forgotten?

Here the teacher says the phrase *Was meinst du?* very quickly and leaves off the *–st* ending.

T. Was mein– du? *Was habe ich vergessen?*	*Was mein– du?* What have I forgotten?
C. *Sie haben –st vergessen!*	You have forgotten –st.

What is the ending?

T. *Was ist die Du-Endung?*	What is the *Du*-ending?
C. *Also, sie ist –st.*	Erh it is –st.

▪ Stage 4: Why is it …? It is … because …

The final stage is to start to guide the class into exploring **why** something is as it is. This brings us to point 4 on our continuum.

Why is it wrong?

The teacher gives the class the phrase but with an incorrect ending on the verb and asks not only if this is correct or not, but also requires the appropriate answer to be given along with an explanation.

T. Was meine Du? *Ist das richtig?*	*Was meine Du?* Is that correct?
C. *Nein, das ist falsch. Es ist* Was meinst du? *und nicht* Was meine du? *–e ist die falsche Endung!*	No. That is wrong. It is *Was meinst du?* and not *Was meine du?* *–e* is the wrong ending.

Why is it that colour?

T. *Warum ist das –st grün?*	Why is the –st green?
C. *Weil es eine Verbendung ist. Was ist ein Verb? Wer kann das Konzept*	Because it is a verb ending. What is a verb? Who can define

Verb definieren?	what a verb is?
C. *Ein Verb ist ein Aktionswort.*	A verb is an action word.
T. *Wer kann ein Beispiel von einem Aktionswort geben?*	Who can give an example of an action word?
P. *Ich gehe ist ein Aktionswort.*	*Ich gehe* is an action word.
T. *Andere Beispiele … ?*	Who can give other examples?
C. *Ich fahre, ich singe u.s.w.*	Ich fahre, ich singe, etc.

- By now, you will have noticed that quite a lot of metalanguage is creeping into the pupils' active vocabulary. How are they able to use this terminology? One reason is because they have been gradually led into an understanding of the concepts, not just the words, underpinning a particular metalinguistic term. Their awareness that verbs may have different endings has gradually been built up and then reinforced in the earlier stages. Stories such as this also help make the grammatical concepts clearer, more vivid and therefore easier to remember.

A. *Guten Tag! Ich bin ein Verb. Ich bin das Verb ‚singen'.*	Hello! I'm a verb. I'm the verb 'singen' *(to sing).*
B. *Wie geht's, Herr Singen?*	How are you, Mr. Singen?
A. *Mir geht's sehr schlecht!*	I'm not well at all!
B. *Warum?*	Why's that?
A. *Ich bin alleine und ich habe keine Endung!*	I'm all alone and I haven't got an ending!
B. *Das tut uns Leid.*	We're sorry to hear that.
A. *Ich muss ein Subjekt finden.*	I have to find a subject.
B. *Ein was? Was ist ein ‚Subjekt'?*	A what? What's a 'subject'?
A. *Ein Subjekt ist eine Person, die ein Verb kontrolliert. ‚Ich' und ‚du' sind Subjekte.*	A subject is a person that controls a verb. 'I' and 'you' are subjects.
B. *Keine Panik auf der Titanic! Hier ist ein ‚ich'!*	No panic on the Titanic! Here's an 'I'!
A. *Danke schön! Ich bin jetzt so glücklich! Ich kann funktionieren! Ich singe!*	Thank you very much! Now I'm so happy! I can work! I am singing!

As always, however, pupils will also need to practise the new terminology. The OHT in Figure 5.8. was used as the basis for a pretend heated argument in a role play. Clearly the definition of a verb offered here is inaccurate. *To become, to effect, to be* hardly call to mind actions. Yet we have to start somewhere and these are 'prototype' rules which gradually evolve in their complexity with pupils being encouraged to spot exceptions and refine them.

```
Dans une phrase, il y a
un nom, un adjectif et un verbe.
· Un quoi ?!
· Un verbe !
· Un quoi ?
· Un verbe !
· C'est quoi, un verbe ?
· Un verbe représente une action.
  Une quoi?
· Une action!
· Une quoi?
· Une action!
· Quelle sorte d'action?
· Par exemple, écouter, nager, jouer,
  finir, descendre
```

Figure 5.8. Visual support for terminology

Handing the discussion over to the pupils

So far, much of the interaction that has taken place is clearly dominated by the teacher and the analogy with performing seals again presents itself. As is true with most areas of language learning, it is not only possible but also important for pupils to undertake independently almost anything that the teacher undertakes; the *teacher clone technique* referred to in chapter 2.

The first two examples below are teach-and-test activities involving a Year 10 middle set who have been learning German for two years. However, it is only now with a new teacher, in fact a student teacher, that they are starting to explore grammar explicitly.

Again the process is gradual. Thus with the gender of nouns, discussed in the homework example earlier, pupils began by associating colours with the appropriate gender. Partner work was then used, with pupils shutting their eyes so they could not see the pictures on the 'gender display' walls. Typical interaction was:

Example 1

A. *Also, du hast eine Minute und du musst mir sagen, ob der oder die.*	A. O.K., you've got one minute and you have to tell me whether it's *der* or *die* (the).
Bahnhof	Railway station
B. *Der.*	B. *Der.*
Am Ende:	At the end:
A. *Halt! Du hast:*	A. Stop! You got:
15 richtig gesagt.	15 right.
12 richtig und 3 falsch gesagt.	12 right and 3 wrong.
Alles richtig gesagt.	All of them right.
Alles richtig gesagt, und zwar 18.	All of them right, that's 18.

The next teach-and-test game had to be played against the clock.

Example 2

A. *Warum ist ‚Park' blau?*	A. Why is '*Park*' blue?
B. *Weil es ein ‚der' Wort ist.*	B. Because it's a '*der*' (definite article, masculine) word.
A. *Warum ist ‚Disko' rot?*	A. Why is '*Disko*' red?
B. *Weil es ein ‚die' Wort ist.*	B. Because it's a '*die*' (feminine) word.
A. *Warum ist ‚Restaurant' grün?*	A. Why is '*Restaurant*' green?
B. *Weil es ein ‚das' Wort ist.*	B. Because it's a '*das*' (neuter) word.
A. *Nochmal! Du musst schneller reagieren!*	A. Again! You have to react faster!

The next examples are actual transcriptions from a Year 10 'beginner' class but this is a high-attaining group. At the time the recordings were made, they had been learning German for about sixty hours with an experienced teacher with a commitment to this approach. He has made a point of stressing, from the outset, the language of interaction across a whole range of classroom routines, as well as within the specific sphere of discussing grammar. In these extracts, pupils in groups are discussing sentences from their homework, written on the board. Some of them contain mistakes. The pupils have to work out which sentences are correct, which are wrong and why. The only support provided is the list of sentences itself.

Extract 1

Here the pupils have decided that *Wo ist den Bahnhof?/Where is the station?* is incorrect. (The accusative ending has been used on the article instead of the nominative.) They are now explaining why.

Rachel: *Kannst du das erklären?*	Can you explain this?
Jenny: *Weil* ist *in der Satz ist und* Bahnhof *ist das Subjekt.*	Because *ist* is in the sentence and *Bahnhof* is the subject.
T: *Was ist ein Subjekt überhaupt?*	What do you actually mean by 'subject'?
Jenny: *Ein Subjekt ist entweder ein Ding, das das Verb kontrolliert oder eine Person, die das Verb kontrolliert.*	A subject is either a thing which controls the verb or a person who controls the verb.

Extract 2

The sentence being corrected in this extract is:

Dann geht er nach unten, trinken Tee und essen Toast dazu.

The French equivalent would be:

Puis, il va en bas, il boire du thé et il manger du toast.

Rachel: *Nummer sieben, Faye.*	Number seven, Faye.
Faye: *Dann geht er nach unten, trinken Tee und essen Toast dazu. Das ist falsch, weil das Verbendung falsch ist.*	*Dann geht er nach unten, trinken Tee und essen Toast dazu.* That's wrong, because the verb ending is wrong.
Rachel and others in group: *Warum?*	Why?
Faye: *Warum? Das Subjekt ist er, deshalb das Verb ... wie heisst* 'should be'?	Why? The subject is *er*, that's why the verb .... how do you say 'should be'?
Jenny: ‚*Sollte sein‘.*	'Should be'.
Faye: *Es sollte ‚trinkt Tee und isst Toast‘ und nicht ‚trinken Tee und essen Toast‘ sein.*	It should be *trinkt Tee und isst Toast* and not *trinken Tee und essen Toast*.

Others in group: *Ja. Das geht.*	Yes. That's correct,
Jenny: *Wir verstehen.*	We understand.

The transcriptions suggest that the pupils in this class are not only developing effective insights into how language works, they are also using language spontaneously and language that is highly applicable to many other areas of communication (*Why? Because. Should be. Therefore.*). So, the level of language achieved would have a high surrender value in examination terms – a fact that has to be reassuring when assessing whether it is worth taking the risk of discussing grammar in the target language.

You may be wondering how pupils moved from giving simple explanations that something was **a verb ending/right/wrong** to using the more complex structure of saying what it **should be.** This language of correction and explanation contains within it chunks of language which themselves form excellent contexts for future grammatical exploration and can quite feasibly reach level 6 or 7 of Attainment Target 2 in the National Curriculum. In a sense, the language involved in even the most complicated examples can be no more difficult than saying the type of pet you have and why you like it. When we were at school, we may not have tackled the pluperfect subjunctive until the Sixth Form. We only used such language when we were able to talk about it in explicit grammatical terms. In short, the explicit preceded the implicit. But there is no reason why we should not provide our pupils with the opportunity to use language such as this much earlier in their language learning careers. The only difference is that they will be using it as an *unanalysed chunk.* The flow diagram below represents a possible route of progression.

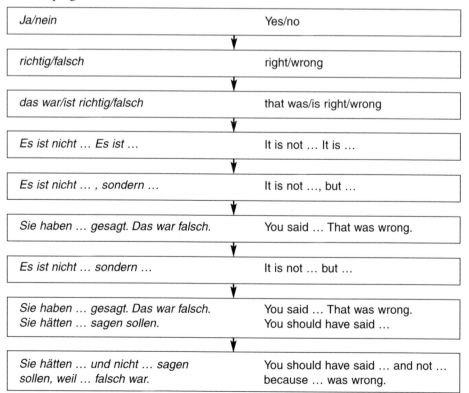

Ja/nein	Yes/no
richtig/falsch	right/wrong
das war/ist richtig/falsch	that was/is right/wrong
Es ist nicht ... Es ist ...	It is not ... It is ...
Es ist nicht ... , sondern ...	It is not ..., but ...
Sie haben ... gesagt. Das war falsch.	You said ... That was wrong.
Es ist nicht ... sondern ...	It is not ... but ...
Sie haben ... gesagt. Das war falsch. Sie hätten ... sagen sollen.	You said ... That was wrong. You should have said ...
Sie hätten ... und nicht ... sagen sollen, weil ... falsch war.	You should have said ... and not ... because ... was wrong.

- We have just seen how in German the language exponents that express a specific function can become ever increasingly complex over a period of time (from *it is wrong* to *you should have said …*). The key to this increasing complexity is careful planning. You might like to work out a similar progression for French or Spanish.

Conclusion

Can we afford to take the risk?

Let us return to the issue of the risks involved in taking time to exploit the language of spontaneous classroom interaction; whether in the presentation and practice stages, described in chapter 2, or in the guided language production and problem-solving tasks illustrated in chapters 3 and 4, or in classroom routines and the explicit teaching of grammar discussed in this chapter.

It is perhaps fitting that the final comment in this book on whether such activities do yield an acceptable dividend in terms of improved linguistic progression and strategic competence is left to the judgement of a pupil. The transcription below is an extract from a 25 minutes conversation with Frances, now in the Sixth Form. She started learning German in the Year 10 beginner class, described above and is now in Year 13. Someone she has never met before, a student teacher, questions her in German about **how** she learnt German. We recognise that in many ways she represents the ideal pupil – a thoughtful, perceptive and highly motivated learner. Nevertheless, she alights on many of the key themes within this book that we believe are applicable to all our pupils. From the discussion, we see the value of:

- catering for the range of ways in which individuals learn languages;
- personalising the learning process;
- providing pupils with the means, the opportunities and the confidence to interrupt, question and even contradict the teacher;
- balancing fluency and accuracy;
- balancing new intuitive and experiential language learning with opportunities for analysis and reflection;
- a gradual, graded approach to the teaching of grammar, which encourages pupils to work out for themselves how the grammar functions;
- pupils reflecting on and understanding the learning process and taking some responsibility for it.

Hopefully Frances's thoughts, coupled with the results of the various projects described in the book, may help you to arrive at a final conclusion that 'the game really is worth the candle'.

Ian: Also, ist es nicht einfacher Grammatik auf English zu machen? Ich würde meinen ,ja, machen wir das auf Englisch'.	So, is it not easier to do grammar in English? I would think 'yes we'll do this in English'.

Frances: Ich glaube vielleicht für den Lehrer ist es einfacher ...

I think perhaps it's easier for the teacher ...

Ian: Hast du viel Arbeit mit Verben gemacht?

Did you do much work with verbs?

Frances: Ja, ich glaube ... wir haben es ziemlich langsam gemacht. Zuerst haben wir nur ich und du. ,Wie heißt du? Ich heiße Frances'.

Yes I think ... we did it fairly slowly. At first we only have *ich* and *du*. *Wie heißt du? Ich heiße Frances.*

Ian: Wie hast du das gelernt, zum Beispiel?

How did you learn that, for example?

Frances: Mit Mimen.

With actions.

Ian: Mit Mimen?

With actions?

Frances: Ja.

Yes.

Ian: Kannst du ein Beispiel geben?

Can you give an example?

Frances: OK ... zum Beispiel, Ich wohne, du wohnst, er,sie, es wohnt, wir wohnen, sie wohnen, Sie wohnen. [Frances does mimes for each conjugation, emphasising the verb ending and the subject]

OK ... for example, *Ich wohne, du wohnst, er, sie, es wohnt, wir wohnen, sie wohnen, Sie wohnen.* [Frances does actions for each conjugation, emphasising the verb ending and the subject]

Ian: Interessant, und das hast du mit Mimen gemacht?

Interesting, and you did that with actions?

Frances: Ja, und das ist ziemlich gut für kinästhetische Lerner zum Beispiel.

Yes, and that is good for kinaesthetic learners, for example.

Ian: Kinästhetik?

Kinaesthetic?

Frances: Sie lernen, ja, durch Mimen. Sie müssen etwas tun.

They learn through actions. They must do something.

Ian: Solche Menschen gibt es?

Are there many people like this?

Frances: Ja, ziemlich viele Menschen.

Yes, quite a few people.

Ian: Und sind alle Lerner so?

And are all learners like this?

Frances: Nicht alle Lerner. Es gibt doch auditive Lerner und visuelle Lerner. Visuelle Lerner, sie müssen etwas sehen. Sie finden es leichter zu schreiben und zu lesen als zu sprechen und zu hören, und, ja, sie sind ziemlich ordentlich. Und auditive Lerner, sie müssen etwas hören und sprechen. Sie

Not all learners. There are auditory learners and visual learners. Visual learners, they must see something. They find it easier to write and to read than to speak and listen, and, yes, they are fairly organised. And auditory learners, they must hear

sind ein bisschen chaotisch und ziemlich
leicht abzulenken, würde ich sagen.

Ian: Und waren dann deine Deutschstunden,
waren sie auch sehr interaktiv oder so?
Hast du immer viele Fragen stellt?

Frances: Ja, natürlich. Immer.

Ian: Was für Fragen, zum Beispiel?

Frances: Das ist, ja, sehr schwer zu
erinnen, jetzt. Wir mussten sagen ‚Wie heißt
das? Was ist die Bedeutung? Ich kann das
nicht verstehen‘. Wir mussten immer sagen
das und, ja, wir mussten die Grammatik
sagen ‚Warum ist es so?‘ Und …

Ian: Warum? Hat dein Lehrer das nicht
erklärt, oder so?

Frances: Ich glaube, daß er dachte, daß
es besser sein würde, wenn wir das
definieren könnten, und ich glaube, ja, ich
kann das erinnen, daß vielleicht ein
Mädchen, sie hat etwas gemacht und
diese Definition oder Erklärung ist immer
mit diesem Mädchen in meiner Erinnerung
und das ist noch eine Verbindung zu haben.

Ian: Was meinst du mit ‚Verbindung‘? Kannst
du ein Beispiel geben?

Frances: Vielleicht, ja, … wie ich schon mal
gesagt habe, es gibt ein Mädchen. Sie
heißt Clare und sie hat diese Regel mit
Nebensatz oder Hauptsatz und sie hat das
gesagt und das war immer ihre Idee und zwar
denke ich, wenn ich von Nebensätze und
so weiter denke, denke ich auch an Clare.

Ian: Ach so … Was meinst du damit mit
‚Hauptsatz‘ und ‚Nebensatz‘?

Frances: Also, ein Hauptsatz kann allein
stehen aber ein Nebensatz kann nicht allein
existieren, weil es keinen Sinn haben würde.

Ian: Wie ist es mit der englischen Grammatik?

something and speak. They are a
little chaotic and fairly easy to distract,
I would say.

And so were your German lessons,
were they also very interactive? Did
you always ask lots of questions?

Yes, of course. Always.

What sort of questions, for example?

That is very difficult to remember now.
We had to say Wie heißt das? Was
ist die Bedeutung? Ich kann das
nicht verstehen. We always had to
say that and, yes, with grammar we
had to say Warum ist es so? And …

Why? Had your teacher not explained
it, or what?

I think that he thought that it would
be better if we could define it, and
I think, yes, I can remember that a
girl, perhaps, she did something and
this definition or explanation is always
with this girl in my memory and that
is still a connection.

What do you mean, 'connection'?
Can you give an example?

Perhaps, yes … as I said before, there
is a girl. She is called Clare and she
has this rule about main clause and
subordinate clause and that was
always her idea and, in fact, when I
think of subordinate clauses I think
of Clare.

I see … what do you mean by 'main
clause' and 'subordinate clause'?

Well, a main clause can stand on its
own, but a subordinate clause cannot
exist on its own because it would
make no sense.

What about English grammar?

Frances: Aber mit Englisch ist es ein bisschen schwerer, weil ich mache das total implizit. Ich weiß nicht die Regeln, weil ich das total instinktiv mache. In Deutsch sage ich das instinktiv, aber ich weiß auch, was die Regeln sind.

But with English it is a bit harder because I do it totally implicitly. I do not know the rules because I do it totally instinctively. In German I say it instinctively, but I also know what the rules are.

Bibliography

BBC (1988) 'Vive la différence' in BBC Learning Zone: Teaching MFL; Part 1.

Brown, K. and Brown, M. (1996) *New Contexts for Modern Language Learning; Cross-curricular Approaches.* London: CILT.

Canale, M. (1983) 'From communicative competence to communicative language pedagogy'. In J. Richards and R. Schmidt (eds.) *Language and Communication.* Harlow: Longman.

Charis Project, Français (1997) Nottingham: The Stapleford Centre.

Clark, J. and Hamilton, J. (1984) *Syllabus Guidelines for a Graded Communicative Approach towards School Foreign Language Learning.* London: CILT.

Council for Cultural Co-operation Education Committee, Modern Languages Division, Strasbourg (2001) Common European Framework of Reference for Languages: Learning, teaching, asessment. Cambridge University Press.

Coyle, D. (1999) 'The next stage? Is there a future for the present? The legacy of the "communicative approach"'. Francophonie 19: 13-16.

Cummins, J. (1984) *Bilingualism and Special Education: Issues in Assessment and Pedagogy.* Clevedon: Multilingual Matters

Dam, L. (1995) *Learner Autonomy 3: From Theory to Classroom Practice.* Dublin: Authentik.

Department for Education and Employment (1999) *Modern Foreign Languages in the National Curriculum.* London: HMSO.

Dobson, A. (1998) *MFL Inspected. Reflections on Inspection Findings 1996/7.* London: CILT.

Dörnyei, Z. (1995) 'On the teachability of communication strategies'. *TESOL Quarterly,* 29, 1: 55–80.

Dörnyei, Z. and Csizér, K. (1998) 'Ten commandments for motivating language learners: results of an empirical study'. *Language Teaching Research* 2 (3): 203–229.

Grenfell, M. and Harris, V. (1993) 'How do pupils learn? Part 1'. *Language Learning Journal* 8: 22–25.

Grenfell, M. (1994) 'Communication. Sense and nonsense'. In Swarbrick, A. (ed.) *Teaching Modern Languages.* London: Routledge in association with the Open University.

Hamilton, J. and McLeod, A. (1993) *Drama in the Languages Classroom.* London: CILT.

Hawkins, E. (1987) *Modern Languages in the Curriculum.* Cambridge: Cambridge University Press.

Johnstone, R. (1989) *Communicative Interaction: a Guide for Language Teachers.* London: CILT.

McDonough, S. H. (1999) 'Learner Strategies: State of the art article'. *Language Teaching* 32: 1–18.

McNab, R. and Barrabé, F. (1993) *Avantage 2.* Oxford: Heinemann.

Mitchell, R. and Martin, C. (1997) 'Rote learning, creativity and "understanding" in classroom foreign language teaching'. *Language Teaching Research* 1 (1): 1–27.

Page, B. (1992) *Letting Go – Taking Hold.* London: CILT.

Skehan, P. and Foster, P. (1997) 'Task type and task processing conditions as influences on foreign language performance'. *Language Teaching Research* 1(3): 185–211.

Skehan, P. (1998) *A cognitive approach to Language Learning.* Oxford: Oxford University Press.

Vandergrift, L. and Bélanger, C. (1998) 'The national core French assessment project: design and field test of formative evaluation instruments at the Intermediate level'. *The Canadian Modern Language Review,* 54, (4): 553–578

Willis, J. (1996) *A Framework for Task-Based Learning.* Harlow: Longman.